Pass **ECDL4**

Module 1: Concepts of Information Technology
Module 2: Using the Computer and Managing Files

Using Microsoft Windows XP

R.P. Richards

Published by

PAYNE-GALLWAY

P U B L I S H E R S   L T D

An imprint of Harcourt Education Ltd.
Halley Court, Jordan Hill, Oxford OX2 8EJ

www.payne-gallway.co.uk

Acknowledgements

We are grateful to the following organisations for granting us permission to reproduce articles, screenshots and photographs:

Intel Corporation

Sun Microsystems

Every effort has been made to contact copyright owners of material published in this book. We would be glad to hear from unacknowledged sources at the earliest opportunity.

Cover design by Direction Advertising and Design Ltd

First Edition 2004

10 09 08 07 06
10 9 8 7 6 5 4 3 2

A catalogue entry for this book is available from the British Library.

10-digit ISBN: 1 904467 30 X

13-digit ISBN: 978 1 904467 30 4

Copyright © R.P. Richards 2004

The ECDL Trade Mark is the registered trade mark of The European Computer Driving Licence Foundation Limited in Ireland and other countries.

This ECDL Foundation approved courseware product incorporates learning reinforcement exercises. These exercises are included to help the candidate in their training for the ECDL. The exercises included in this courseware product are not ECDL certification tests and should not be construed in any way as ECDL certification tests. For information about Authorised ECDL Test Centres in different National Territories please refer to the ECDL Foundation web site at www.ecdl.com

All rights reserved

Printed in Malta by Gutenberg Press

Disclaimer

Preface

Who is this book for?

This book is suitable for anyone studying for ECDL Version 4.0 (Modules 1 and 2), either at school, adult class or at home. It is suitable for complete beginners or those with some prior experience.

The approach

Module 1 is a theoretical module which explains basic concepts of hardware and software. In Module 2, the approach is very much one of "learning by doing". The module is divided into a number of chapters which correspond to one lesson. The student is guided step-by-step through a practical task at the computer, with numerous screenshots to show exactly what should be on their screen at each stage. Each individual in a class can proceed at their own pace, with little or no help from a teacher. At the end of most chapters there are exercises which provide invaluable practice. By the time a student has completed a module, every aspect of the ECDL syllabus for that module will have been covered.

Software used

The text and screenshots are based on a PC running Microsoft Windows XP and Microsoft Office 2003. However, it will be relatively easy to adapt the instructions for use with earlier versions.

Extra resources

Answers to practice exercises and other useful supporting material can be found on the publisher's web site www.payne-gallway.co.uk/ecdl.

About ECDL

The European Computer Driving Licence (ECDL) is the European-wide qualification enabling people to demonstrate their competence in computer skills. Candidates must study and pass the test for each of the seven modules listed below before they are awarded an ECDL certificate. The ECDL tests must be undertaken at an accredited test centre. For more details of ECDL tests and test centres, visit the ECDL web site www.ecdl.com.

Module 1: Concepts of Information Technology

Module 2: Using the Computer and Managing Files

Module 3: Word Processing

Module 4: Spreadsheets

Module 5: Database

Module 6: Presentation

Module 7: Information and Communication

Module 1
Concepts of Information Technology

This module will give you an understanding of some of the main concepts of IT at a general level. You will learn about:

- types of computers and the component parts of a computer
- types of software and the uses of software applications in everyday life
- how computer networks are used, including the use of the Internet, e-mail and e-commerce
- health and safety issues relevant to the use of computers
- security issues arising from the use of computers
- legislation such as the Data Protection Act and legal issues regarding copyright

Module 1   Table of Contents

General Concepts

A world of computers

In this module you'll be learning about what a computer is and about some of the thousands of ways in which computers are used today. Amazingly, the history of commercial computing goes back only to around 1960, when the first computers were used by a very few large organisations to perform repetitive tasks such as processing the company payroll. These computers were massive, occupying whole floors in office blocks, and yet had only a fraction of the computing power of a modern pocket calculator. The computer that controlled the first manned spaceship to the moon in 1969 had less calculating capability than a mobile phone in 2003!

The term **Information Technology** (IT) has been coined to refer to the use of computers, and machines like fax machines and telephones which contain tiny computers, to process and transfer information. Computers are now commonly used to communicate information, as well as performing tasks like word processing or calculations. You may often hear the term **ICT** or **Information and Communication Technology** used instead of **IT**.

Hardware and software

In order to work, a computer needs two things – hardware and software.

Hardware is the physical part of a computer – the bits you can see and touch. The casings for computers and their associated pieces of hardware such as monitors and printers are usually made of tough plastic. The hardware inside the casings is made up of electronic switches and integrated circuits (commonly known as 'chips') mounted on boards (**printed circuit boards** or **PCBs**).

Software is the list of instructions that are coded in a special way so the computer can understand them. These computer **programs** tell the computer exactly what to do. There are many different types of program – for example:

❶   **applications software** such as a word processor or an e-mail package.

❶   **operating system software** such as Windows which works away in the background and lets you decide which applications software to run.

Many common household devices such as washing machines, microwave ovens, video recorders and digital alarm clocks contain computer hardware and specialised software to make them perform the tasks they are designed to do.

Types of computer

Different types of computers are used for different applications.

Mainframe computers are large, fast and expensive. They are used by very big organisations such as electricity companies, banks or multinational companies. Hundreds or thousands of users may be connected to and using a mainframe at the same time.

Each user has a **computer terminal** that is connected to the mainframe. Some types of terminal cannot be used for anything unless they are connected to the mainframe – these are known as **dumb terminals**. All the computer's calculations take place in the mainframe. Alternatively, an ordinary PC may be connected to a mainframe and this can do useful work even if it is not connected at any particular time. A PC used in this way is sometimes known as an **intelligent terminal**.

The terminals connected to a mainframe computer may be in different parts of the country, or even overseas.

A **network** computer (normally referred to as a network **server**) has a number of personal computers connected to it to create a computer network. The server is typically used to store information for use by all the users on the network.

Personal computers

A **personal computer** or **PC** has become an almost indispensable piece of equipment for office workers from the managing director down to the humblest clerical worker.

The most popular type of PC is the **desktop model**. The main **system unit** is designed to sit on top of the user's desk. **Tower models** are also popular as the system unit can be sited on the floor, so taking up less desk space.

The picture below shows the main parts of a desktop PC:

Speakers:
These allow you to listen to music and other sounds from your computer.

Screen:
This displays information from the computer.

System unit:
This contains the CPU (Central Processing Unit), hard disk drive, removable disk drives and memory.

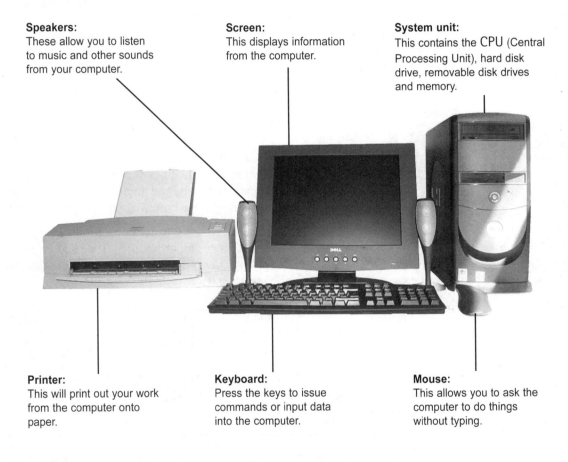

Printer:
This will print out your work from the computer onto paper.

Keyboard:
Press the keys to issue commands or input data into the computer.

Mouse:
This allows you to ask the computer to do things without typing.

Tip:
Hardware devices such as the screen, keyboard, mouse etc. connected to the main system unit are often referred to as **peripherals**.

Portable computers were introduced so that users could easily transport their PC to different locations and even do some work en route, perhaps on a train journey. There are two main types:

Notebook computers (sometimes called laptop computers) are portable computers that have an integral keyboard and monitor and a rechargeable battery.

Palmtops are really small and, as their name suggests, can fit in the palm of your hand. They are becoming more and more powerful as the technology improves. Some palmtops allow the user to draw on the screen with a special pen – the drawings are then converted into text and diagrams.

A **PDA** or Personal Digital Assistant is a handheld computer which can also be used as a mobile phone. The PDA began as an electronic organiser, after the success of the paper-based Filofax in the mid-1980s. The handheld device looks very much like a calculator. Recent models include spellcheckers, small games and notepad functions, and some models with larger screens now have handwriting-recognition software.

PDAs tend to fall into two categories; keyboard- and pen-based devices. Both types of devices have similar features. They sometimes have a headset if being used as a telephone. They have cut-down versions of PC applications and can be easily connected to a PC to transfer data.

	Capacity	Speed	Cost	Typical users
Mainframe	Very large disk storage. Very large main memory	Very fast in order to process vast amounts of data	Extremely expensive	Large companies (often multinational), Health Authorities etc.
Network server	Large disk storage (now measured in Gigabytes (Gb). Large main memory (RAM)	Fast - measured in GHz	Expensive due to components and software for networking functions, backup etc.	Smaller companies, schools, hospitals etc.
PC	Probably smaller disk storage and main memory (RAM) than a server (especially if networked)	Fast - measured in GHz	Becoming cheaper all the time.	Employees wthin all sizes of organisation, home users etc.
Laptop	Similar to a PC	Similar to a PC	Often more expensive than for a comparably powered PC due to miniaturisation of components	Mostly business users, commuters etc.
PDA	Much smaller disk storage capacity and main memory than a PC	Slower than a PC	Relatively expensive compared to a PC	Mostly business users, commuters etc.

Hardware

Central Processing Unit

Within the system unit the main brain of the computer is the **Central Processing Unit** (CPU). This is where all processing and calculations take place. It consists of two different parts:

- ❶ The processor
- ❶ Memory

The processor

The processor consists of two main components – the **control unit** and the **arithmetic/logic unit** (ALU). The control unit fetches instructions from the computer's memory, decodes them and synchronises all the computer's operations.

The **arithmetic/logic unit** (ALU) is where all of the work is carried out. The ALU can perform two sorts of operations on data. **Arithmetic** operations include addition, subtraction, multiplication and division. **Logical** operations consist of comparing one data item with another to determine whether the first data item is smaller than, equal to or greater than the second data item.

Physically the processor is a small silicon **chip**, which consists of complex electronic circuits. This chip, together with other chips that do different jobs, are mounted on **printed circuit boards** (PCBs).

Computer memory

A computer has a 'memory' which stores information. There are two kinds of memory: **Random Access Memory** (RAM) and **Read-Only Memory** (ROM).

RAM (sometimes known as **immediate access memory**) is divided into millions of addressable storage units called **bytes**.

Each byte consists of 8 bits or binary digits. A bit can be set either ON or OFF, depending on whether an electric current is switched on or off, representing a 0 or a 1. All numbers, text, sounds, graphics etc are held as different patterns of 0s and 1s in the computer.

One byte can hold one character, or it can be used to hold a code representing, for example, a tiny part of a picture, a sound, or part of a computer program instruction. The total number of bytes in main memory is referred to as the computer's memory size.

Computer memory sizes are measured using the following units:

Measurement	Power of 2	Size (bytes)	Symbol
1 Kilobyte	2^{10}	1,024 (just over 1 thousand)	Kb
1 Megabyte	2^{20}	1,048,576 (just over 1 million)	Mb
1 Gigabyte	2^{30}	1,073,741,824 (just over 1 billion)	Gb
1 Terabyte	2^{40}	1,099,511,627,776 (just over 1 trillion)	Tb

So for example this paragraph contains approximately 180 characters or bytes. The text in this module is stored as a **file** which contains approximately 60,000 characters (approximately 59 kb). Files are organised into **directories** or **folders**. Files and folders are given names so that they can easily be found on the computer.

The amount of memory that comes with a standard PC has increased exponentially over the past 20 years. In about 1980, BBC microcomputers with 32K of memory were bought in their thousands for home and school use. In 1981, Bill Gates of Microsoft made his famous remark "640K ought to be enough for anybody". By 2003, a PC with 256Mb or 512Mb of memory was standard, costing less than £1,000 including bundled software.

Instructions and data being processed are held in **RAM**. If you are writing a letter using MS Word, for example, both Word and your letter will be held in RAM while you are working on it. If you accidentally switch off the machine, or there is a power cut while you are working, you will lose the letter if you have not saved it and when you restart the computer, you will have to load Word again. (i.e. the MS Word software will be copied from your hard disk into RAM). When you finish your letter, save it and close Word, RAM is freed up for the next task.

RAM has these two major characteristics:

❶   Each location in RAM has its own unique address. It can be randomly accessed – the computer can be instructed to fetch the data it needs from any given address in memory.

❷   RAM is **volatile** – its contents are lost when the power is switched off.

A PC will also only have a very small amount of **ROM**. Unlike RAM, its contents can never be changed, and all the instructions held in ROM have to be burned into the memory chip before it leaves the factory. The contents of ROM are not lost when the computer is switched off. The tiny program which starts running as soon as you switch the computer on is held in ROM. This program tells the computer to start loading the operating system (e.g. Windows) from disk.

ROM has these two major characteristics:

❶   ROM cannot be written to or used to hold ordinary user application programs such as word processing software.

❷   ROM is **non-volatile** – its contents are NOT lost when the power is switched off.

Tip:

> Many household machines contain ROM chips - for example your washing machine, dishwasher or video recorder. You can, for example, select which washing program to use, but you cannot change how many minutes the cycle takes or use the washing machine to cook your dinner instead!

Computer performance

Two main factors impact on a computer's performance: **processor speed** and **amount of RAM**.

Processor speed is measured in **kilohertz** or **gigahertz**. (1GHz is equal to one million KHz.)

Each year, as technology advances, processor speed increases. Twenty years ago a computer with a processor speed of a few hundred kilohertz (KHz) would have been considered very powerful. Now a processor speed of 1.8GHz is not unusual – that is about 10,000 times faster!

 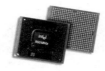 

The other factor in determining the performance of a computer is the amount of memory (or **RAM**) it has. Modern software takes up a huge amount of memory.

When you install software such as Microsoft Word on your computer, it is stored on the hard disk inside the system unit, which may have a capacity of anything between say, 10Gb and 160Gb. When you open Word to write a letter, for example, the software program (Word) has to be copied into RAM (which may have a capacity of say, 256 or 512Mb) before the computer can execute the program instructions which enable you to type your letter.

If a computer does not have enough memory to hold all of Microsoft Word in memory (RAM) at once, it will swap bits of the program in and out of memory from disk as they are required. This takes time.

The same happens when you have several programs running at once. They all take up memory space, and your computer may run more slowly because instructions and data are being copied from disk to memory as needed.

Thus, the **number of applications** running at any one time also affects the performance of a computer.

Input devices

All the data that is fed *into* a computer is called **input**. The items of hardware used to input data are called **input devices**. These are some of the most common input devices:

Keyboard

The most common way to enter data into a PC is by **keyboard**. Computer keyboards have their keys arranged in a similar way to those on a typewriter. This way of arranging keys is called QWERTY because of the order in which the keys appear in the first row of letters. Extra keys carry out specific jobs depending on the software being used.

Some keyboards, especially on laptop computers, incorporate a **tracker ball** that performs the function of a mouse.

Mouse

A **mouse** is a small hand-held input device which has a ball fitted underneath. When the mouse is moved, the signal created by the movement of the ball is transmitted to the computer. This controls a pointer on the screen which moves in a direction corresponding to the direction of the mouse. Once the user has pointed the arrow on their screen at something it can be selected by clicking a button on top of the mouse. There are usually two or three buttons on a mouse. The left-hand button is normally used to make selections.

Tracker balls are also types of pointing device. They are often used instead of a mouse on portable computers. The user rotates a ball to move the cursor over the screen.

Touch pads can also replace the mouse, they too are often found on the keyboards of portable computers. The user moves their finger over the surface of the pad to move the cursor.

Microphone

If your computer has a sound card it should have the ability to receive sound input from a **microphone** through the sound card microphone port. This may be useful for recording voice or sounds on your computer.

Light pen

A **light pen** is a small pen-shaped wand which contains light sensors. The light pen is used to choose objects or commands on the screen either by pressing it against the screen or by pressing a small switch on its side. This sends a signal to the computer, which then works out the exact location of the light pen on the screen.

Scanner

Scanners are used to input text, diagrams and pictures to the computer. They can be hand-held but usually they are 'flat bed' devices which sit on the desk. Printed text can be scanned using OCR (Optical Character Recognition) software so that it can be word-processed. Images can be scanned and loaded into graphics software where they can be altered or enhanced.

Joystick

A **joystick** is often used to play games on a PC. It controls the way things move on the screen and can control movement from side-to-side, up and down and diagonally. A joystick normally has at least one button that can be used in a game, for example to make a character jump or fire a missile.

Digital camera

A major benefit of using a **digital camera** is that you can transfer photos directly to your PC without sending a film off to be developed. A cable supplied with the camera can connect it to a port on the back of your PC.

Using a digital camera is very similar to using a traditional camera. They both use the basic components such as a lens, flash, shutter and viewfinder. Most digital models now incorporate an LCD screen so that you can get a good view of your subject as you take the photo, and you can then review the picture afterwards.

The quality and number of digital pictures that can be taken will depend on the amount of memory in the camera.

Output devices

The information that a computer produces is called **output**. The items of hardware that receive this output are called **output devices**. The most common output devices are shown below:

Screen

A **screen** (or **monitor**) displays the output information from a computer. The size of a monitor is measured in inches diagonally across the screen; 15, 17, 19 and 21 inch monitors are the most common sizes. The picture on a monitor is made up of thousands of tiny coloured dots called **pixels**.

The quality and detail of the picture on a monitor depends on the **resolution** which is measured in pixels going across and down the screen. The more pixels the screen has, the higher the resolution and the better the picture. Resolutions typically range from 800 x 600 to 1,600 x 1,200. Another factor which affects the quality of the image is its **refresh rate**. This is measured in hertz (Hz) and indicates how many times per second the image on the screen is updated. To avoid flickering images which can lead to eyestrain and headaches, the refresh rate of a monitor should be at least 72Hz.

The most common monitors work in the same way as televisions where electrical signals are converted into an image on the screen by a **Cathode Ray Tube** (CRT).

New flat-screen monitors take up much less desk space than CRTs. These **Liquid Crystal Display** (LCD) screens are similar to those provided on portable computers.

Printer

A good printer can help you produce professional-looking printed output from your PC. There are three main categories of printer, each of them suitable for different types of job.

Many PCs are supplied with an **inkjet** printer. These print pictures or characters by forcing small dots of ink through tiny holes. The ink is stored in replaceable cartridges, normally separate for colour and black ink. These printers can also print on envelopes, labels, acetates and other specialist paper.

Laser printers produce very high quality printed output very quickly. They are suitable for large volume printouts. Colour laser printers are expensive but black and white laser printers cost only a few hundred pounds and are standard in many large and small businesses. The main running expense is the cost of replacement toner (powdered ink) cartridges every few thousand pages.

Dot matrix printers have steel pins which strike an inked ribbon to create a pattern of tiny dots which form a character. How good the print is depends on how many pins the machine has 24 pins will produce better quality print than 9 pins.

This type of printer is not normally supplied with a PC for home use, as the quality is not as good as an inkjet or laser printer. As they work by striking the paper, they are called **impact** printers and are often used by businesses to print on multi-part stationery for producing documents such as invoices. A top copy goes to the customer, a second 'carbon copy' may be used as a delivery note and a third copy may be kept in the office. Laser printers and inkjet printers cannot print two or more copies of a document simultaneously in this way.

Plotter

A **plotter** is another device for producing hard-copy from a computer. It uses several coloured pens to draw the computer output on paper. Plotters can produce very accurate drawings and are often used in Computer-Aided Design (CAD) applications to produce engineering or architectural drawings.

Speakers

External **speakers** are supplied with **multimedia** PCs. These are computers that incorporate a sound card, CD-ROM and speakers. The system can then combine text, sound and graphics to run programs such as games. The quality and volume of the sound produced can be adjusted either within software or on the speakers themselves.

Computers can produce output in the form of sound by using a **speech synthesiser**. This converts electrical signals into sound waves. Sound software can be used to mix musical sounds and create new sounds. Some of the sounds can replicate human speech – this is called speech synthesis which is used by some telephone enquiry systems.

Input/Output devices

Some devices can be classed as input or output devices.

Touchscreen

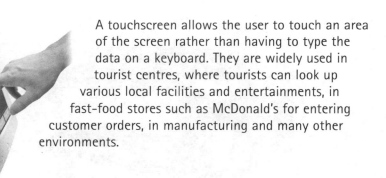

A touchscreen allows the user to touch an area of the screen rather than having to type the data on a keyboard. They are widely used in tourist centres, where tourists can look up various local facilities and entertainments, in fast-food stores such as McDonald's for entering customer orders, in manufacturing and many other environments.

Storage devices

Disk storage

To save your work when the computer is turned off, you need to save it onto a disk. There are three main types of disk: floppy disk, hard disk and CD-ROM.

A **floppy disk** is not floppy at all (although the actual disk is made of flexible plastic). It has a hard protective casing and a storage capacity of 1.44 Mb. You can insert a floppy disk into a computer yourself, store your work on it and then remove it. You could take the disk and insert it into another PC and carry on with your work. Before a floppy disk can be used it must be **formatted**. This means that the disk is checked for errors and set up to accept data. Nowadays the vast majority of floppy disks in the shops are pre-formatted.

A **hard disk** is housed permanently inside your computer. These disks have a much larger storage capacity than a floppy disk, and transfer data to and from computer memory much more quickly.

The capacity of hard disks is measured in megabytes (Mb) or gigabytes (Gb). Most modern PCs have a hard disk with a capacity of at least 10Gb.

PCs are often fitted with a **CD-ROM** (Compact Disk Read Only Memory) drive and speakers. CD-ROMs are removable and can hold large amounts of programs or data. Data is often in the form of text, pictures, music and animations.

New PCs often have the software supplied on CD-ROM and of course it is an ideal medium for games packages. These disks are read-only which means that you cannot save any information on them, only read what is already there. Up to 650Mb of data can be stored on these disks.

CD-RW (read-write) disks save data which can then be erased and overwritten with new data.

DVD drives are also now being supplied as removable storage, allowing you to watch films on your PC. A DVD-ROM can hold up to 135 minutes of high-quality video and CD-quality sound.

Other removable storage

Some PCs are fitted with **Zip** drives. Zip disks are also removable storage media that can be written to as many times as you wish. Newer disks can hold up to 250Mb of data.

A Zip drive is often an option on a PC, together with a CD-ROM or DVD drive and a floppy drive. Alternatively, you can purchase an external disk drive for any of these. While they are faster than floppy disks, they are still much slower than hard disks.

Jaz drives are the big brother of Zip drives; they use similar technology but the disks have a larger capacity of up to 1Gb.

Magnetic tape or **DAT** (Digital Audio tape) is used almost exclusively for backups and for archiving old data that needs to be kept but which will probably never be used. Large amounts of data can be stored very cheaply and compactly using this medium, which is also known as a **data cartridge**. Tapes are much slower to access than a floppy disk, Zip/Jaz disk or CD-ROM.

The table below gives a comparison between the different types of removable PC storage.

Device	Capacity	Price of Drive (approx)	Price of Media (approx)
Floppy Disk	1.44Mb	£25	£0.50
CD	650Mb	£150	£1.00
Jaz	2Gb	£270	£80.00
Zip	250Mb	£150	£10.00
DVD	17Gb	£450	£25.00
DAT	60Gb	£500	£100

Tip:

These prices are changing all the time - only use this table for the sake of comparison.

Exercises

1. A friend tells you that his son's new PC has 100Gb of RAM. Is this plausible? Look up some advertisements for PCs to find a typical figure for RAM and hard disk capacity.

2. Describe **two** differences between RAM and ROM; give a typical use for each.

3. All computers from mainframes to palmtops have certain elements in common, such as a central processing unit (CPU), input, output and storage devices.

   (a) Describe briefly a typical user of each of a **mainframe computer** and a **palmtop**.

   (b) What unit is the speed of the CPU measured in?

   (c) Name the **two** main parts of the CPU and describe the function of each.

4. Explain the terms **Information Technology**, **hardware** and **software**.

5. Describe the functions of each of the following devices and state whether they are input or output devices:

   (a) Touchpad

   (b) Plotter

   (c) Joystick

   (d) Scanner

6. Suppose you have typed a page of text using a word processor. The text contains about 2,000 characters including spaces. Approximately how much RAM will this text occupy?

7. What type of printer would you recommend for each of the following users? Justify your answers.

   (a) An author working at home on her latest novel.

   (b) A small garage printing purchase orders for spare parts. Three copies of each purchase order is required.

   (c) A student who needs to print out his geography project in colour at home.

8. A graphic artist needs to send artwork that he has created on his computer to his client. The graphics files are 50Mb. Name and justify a suitable medium for storing and posting the files.

9. Describe two typical uses of each of the following devices attached to a PC:

   (a) Touch screen

   (b) Speakers

   (c) DVD drive

1.3 Software

Types of software

Computer software programs tell the computer what to do. They are divided into two general areas: systems software and applications software. All software is continually being updated, for example Microsoft Windows 95, 98, 2000 or XP. New programs generally provide more flexibility and features for the user. It is usually possible to upgrade from one version to the next.

Updates to improve the reliability and security of software are often supplied free of charge by the manufacturer. For example Windows Service Pack updates and Office Service Pack (or Release) updates can be downloaded from the Microsoft web site (www.microsoft.com) to keep your PC up-to-date with the latest versions.

It is useful to be aware which software you are working with, since for example you will not be able to open a document created in Word 2002 on a PC with Word 97.

Operating system software

An **operating system** is a series of programs that organise and control a computer. The computer will not work without it. Most PCs use an operating system called **Microsoft Windows**. There have been several versions of Windows and there are bound to be more versions in the future. The main functions of an operating system are:

- To provide a user interface so that the user can communicate with the computer.

- To communicate with all the hardware devices such as keyboard, screen and printer. When the user gives an instruction to print, for example, the operating system checks that the printer is switched on and ready.

- To organise the storage and retrieval of data from disk. The operating system has to keep track of where every file is stored on disk so that it can be retrieved quickly.

- To manage the smooth running of all the programs currently in RAM. The operating system will allocate processing time to each program in turn. For example, while you are thinking what to type into Word, the computer may be busy receiving an e-mail message or saving a spreadsheet you have just been working on.

Graphical User Interface

Windows has a **Graphical User Interface** (GUI). This means that instead of users having to type complicated text commands, they can use the mouse to point at icons and menus on the screen.

> **Tip:**
> A GUI is sometimes called a **WIMP interface** (Windows, Icons, Mouse and Pointer).

> **Tip:**
> Examples of other operating systems include MS-DOS, OS/2, Unix and Linux.

Applications software

Application packages are available for specific tasks. It is up to you to decide which you want on your computer. The most commonly used applications on a PC are Word Processing, Spreadsheets, Databases and Internet/e-mail software.

Word processing software deals mainly with words. You can type all kinds of documents such as letters, CVs, reports etc. When you have finished a document you can print it and save it on a disk. One of the most popular word processing packages is Microsoft Word.

Spreadsheet software deals mainly with numbers. It is very useful for calculations involving money. One of the most popular spreadsheet packages is Microsoft Excel. Most spreadsheet packages are fairly similar in use.

Database software is used to store information about people or items. It allows you to sort the information and find a particular record very quickly. Microsoft Access is one of the most popular database packages.

Internet browser software such as Internet Explorer and Netscape Navigator allows you to surf the World Wide Web. Internet Explorer is supplied as part of Windows and is therefore one of the most popular web browsers.

E-mail software allows you to send messages to other people who have a mailbox e.g. family and friends. Many people use this to keep in touch with family who live abroad. Outlook Express is supplied as part of Windows, and you will probably find this installed on your PC. There are alternatives such as Eudora and Netscape Messenger.

Presentation software helps the user to create visual slide show presentations on a personal computer. These can display text, graphics, limited sound and some animation. The slides can also be printed onto acetates for use in an OHP presentation. Microsoft PowerPoint is often used to produce this type of presentation.

Desktop Publishing such as Microsoft Publisher is used to produce many different types of documents from simple party invitations to more complex applications such as professional-looking newspapers and magazines. Professional users in the publishing industry often use more powerful packages such as QuarkXPress or Pagemaker.

Accounting software helps businesses take control of all bookkeeping and accounting tasks such as calculating VAT returns, producing invoices, tracking cash flow and managing payment and receipts. Sage software is one of the most widely used accounting packages.

Systems development

Computer-based systems are developed by specialist teams of system analysts and programmers. A **systems analyst** analyses the feasibility of a computer system for business, and supervises the design, specification and implementation of the system. A **programmer** writes and tests the computer programs that make up the system. The programmer will be trained to write the programs in a programming language – some you may have heard of include Java, Visual Basic or C++.

The development of large computer-based systems can involve dozens of people working for several months or even years. This means that formal methods and procedures must be applied to ensure that the project is delivered on time and meets the specification. These stages are normally defined, with each stage being completed before the next one begins. The whole process is often known as the **systems life cycle**.

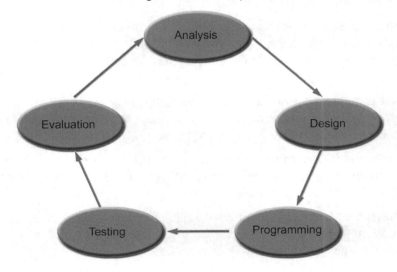

Analysis

When a user has identified a problem or a need for a new computer system, a systems analyst will start by analysing the requirements. For example, what is the expected capacity of the new system? How will information be input into the system? What processing is required? What output is required?

Design

Work now starts on designing the overall system, followed by the detailed design of each subsection. This will include screen layouts, user interfaces, methods of input, defining the format of all the data that needs to be stored, the processing required, and the output in the form of hard copy or on-screen reports.

Programming

The actual programming may be passed out to a team of programmers who will each work on a module of the final package.

Testing

Each module is first tested individually then as part of the whole suite of programs. Special data is prepared for the testing including 'normal' data and erroneous data to make sure that the program will not 'crash', whatever the user enters.

Evaluation

The new system must be evaluated once it has been put into operation to ensure that it is performing as expected.

Sooner or later there will be a perceived need for a new system and the whole process will start all over again.

Exercises

1. (a) Name the two main types of software found on a PC.

   (b) Why are there often several different versions of software packages, each with their own version number? Name an example of some software that has at least two versions.

   (c) Give two reasons why a user may decide to upgrade the software that he is using to the latest version.

2. (a) Explain what is meant by a Graphical User Interface (GUI).

   (b) Give two reasons why a computer user may find a GUI interface easier to use than an alternative where commands have to be typed in.

3. Describe briefly four of the standard development stages in applications software development.

4. Describe briefly the main functions of the operating system.

Information Networks

Local area networks

Although a PC will function perfectly well as a 'standalone' machine, there are many advantages to an organisation of connecting all the computers together into a **network**.

A **local area network** or **LAN** links together via cabling, computers on the same site e.g. within one building. This enables the users connected to the network to share information and to share resources such as printers that are connected to the network. If you are studying on a course at college, you will probably be connected to a LAN.

In a **client/server** network, a powerful computer called a **server** controls the network and stores data which can be used by other computers on the network. The other computers are referred to as **clients**.

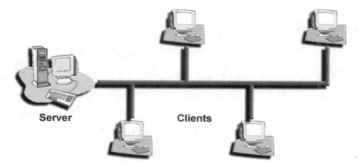

Server   Clients

Advantages of networks

❶   Workstations can share devices like printers. This is cheaper than buying a printer for every workstation.

❶   Users can save their work centrally on the network server. They can then retrieve their work from any workstation on the network.

❶   Users can communicate with each other and transfer data between workstations very easily.

❶   One copy of each application program can be loaded onto the file server and shared by all users. When a new version comes out it only has to be loaded onto the server instead of onto every workstation.

Disadvantages of networks

- ❶ Special security measures are needed to stop users from using programs and data that they shouldn't have access to.

- ❶ Networks are complicated to set up and must be maintained by skilled ICT technicians.

- ❶ If the file server develops a serious fault all the users are affected.

- ❶ If a virus enters the network all the users may be affected.

Wide area networks

A **wide area network** or **WAN** connects computers in different geographical locations all over the world. They are connected using the telephone system. Large multinational companies depend on this type of network to communicate between different parts of their organisations in different countries.

The **Internet** is an example of a worldwide computer network (WAN) made up of smaller networks.

The telephone network in computing

A **modem** is required for communication between computers over telephone lines. This device converts the data from one computer (**digital data** which is a pattern of 0s and 1s) into a form that the telephone system can deal with (**analogue data**) and another modem at the other end will convert the data back into a form that the other computer can understand. The speed at which data is transmitted (the **transfer rate**) is measured in bits per second (**bps**).

PSTN

Short for Public Switched Telephone Network, this is the international telephone system that we are all familiar with for regular telephone calls. It is also referred to as the **Plain Old Telephone Service** (POTS).

ISDN

The amount of data that can be sent over a line depends partly on the bandwidth, which is the range of frequencies that the line can carry. The greater the bandwidth, the greater the rate at which data can be sent, as several messages can be transmitted simultaneously. A network that is capable of sending voice, video and computer data is called an **Integrated Services Digital Network** (ISDN), and this requires a high bandwidth.

ADSL

Asymmetric Digital Subscriber Line (ADSL) is a newer technology which enables existing copper wire telephone lines to be used to transmit computer data at extremely fast rates. The subscriber needs an ADSL modem and two ADSL devices. A 'splitter' (which is a filter), one at the user end and one at the exchange end, separates the telephony signal from the ADSL signal. This means that telephone calls can be made at the same time that data is being sent or received (i.e. a customer can surf the Internet and still make telephone calls).

The Internet

The Internet is a huge number of computers – including yours – connected together all over the world. Using the Internet you can look up information on any subject you can imagine, or send and receive messages through e-mail.

Many people use the Internet to 'surf' the **World Wide Web** – the fastest-growing area of the Internet, made up of millions of web sites.

Every web site consists of one or more documents called pages. A home page is the first page of a web site and serves as an introduction to the whole site. Every page on the web has its own address, called a **Uniform Resource Locator** or **URL**.

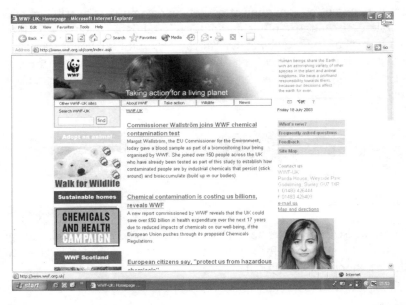

To connect to the Internet you will need a PC with at least a 486 processor and Windows 95 upwards. You will also need a modem installed and connected to a phone outlet. You will then need to choose an **Internet Service Provider** or **ISP** to connect you to the Internet. Many ISPs do not charge for their services (apart from the phone bill) or offer unlimited access for a flat fee. Their software does all the installation for you. There are lots of free trial CDs on offer in high-street shops and magazines.

E-commerce

The growth of the Internet over the past ten years has been phenomenal. In 1989, Tim Berners-Lee introduced the world wide web to his colleagues at CERN. In 1993, there were 130 servers on the web. A year later there were 500. By the beginning of 2003, there were over 35 million.

Virtually every organisation of any size – and a large proportion of small companies – now have their own web sites, and find them as indispensable as the telephone. Everything from travel tickets to office supplies can be purchased over the Internet, often more cheaply than from a High Street store. Online banking is quick, efficient and often cheaper.

Purchasing over the Internet

When you purchase goods over the Internet, you have to enter your name and address. Usually you will also have to enter a credit card number for payment of the goods. The organisation that owns the web site must have a 'secure site' which means that any credit card number that you enter is encrypted, or 'scrambled' in some way, so that it cannot be intercepted. No transaction can be 100% safe but handing your credit card to a waiter in a restaurant is just as risky, if not more so. A consumer who purchases goods over the Internet has the right to return unsatisfactory goods.

Internet shopping has many advantages for the shopper:

❶ The shopping facility is available 24 hours a day, 7 days a week

❶ You don't have to leave home to shop

❶ You can surf the Internet to find the best deal before making a purchase.

However there are some disadvantages:

❶ You cannot see, touch or try on goods before purchasing

❶ You may miss the human contact and advice available in a store

❶ There may be some risk involved in giving a credit card number over the Internet.

Alternative methods of payment

If you are trading online, but don't wish to use a credit card or send cheques through the post there are alternative payment methods. For example NOCHEX (www.nochex.co.uk) allows you to send or receive money from anyone with an e-mail address and a UK debit card. Having opened your NOCHEX account you simply transfer money into it from your bank account or from other NOCHEX users. Similarly you can withdraw money from your bank account to send to retailers. PayPal (www.paypal.com) offer similar facilities.

E-mail

One of the reasons that many people choose to connect to the Internet is e-mail. It has become one of the most popular forms of communication.

Here are some of its advantages over regular mail:

❶   An e-mail message arrives almost instantaneously anywhere in the world

❶   It is very quick and easy to reply to an e-mail, simply by clicking the Reply button and writing a message

❶   The same message can be sent to several people at once

❶   Long documents or photographs can be sent as attachments

❶   A message can easily be forwarded to another person

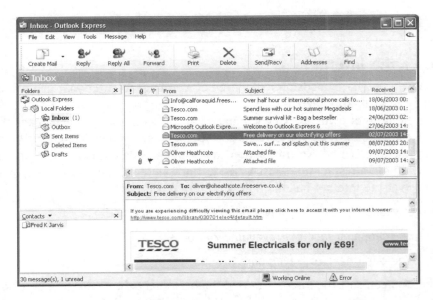

Software such as **Outlook** or **Outlook Express** (above) is needed to send and receive e-mails. The hardware needed is a computer, telephone line and a modem.

Intranets and Extranets

An **intranet** is similar to the Internet but is internal to an organisation, owned and used only by people in the organisation. It allows employees to share information, fix up appointments with each other, circulate important documents internally and many other functions. Remember that in a large organisation not everybody will be working on the same site or even at the same time.

An **extranet** is an intranet that is partially accessible to authorised users. An intranet is accessible only to people who are members of the same company or organisation, an extranet provides various levels of access to users outside of the local network.

You must have a valid username and password to access an extranet and your identity determines which parts of the extranet you can view.

Exercises

1. Explain what is meant by **a client-server network**.

2. (a) Distinguish between a wide area network (WAN) and a local area network (LAN).

   (b) Describe briefly three advantages of connecting PCs into a network rather than using standalone computers.

3. What hardware is needed to connect to the Internet?

4. Name two advantages of ADSL over PSTN for connecting to the Internet.

5. What is the function of a modem?

6. Give 3 advantages and 3 disadvantages of shopping over the Internet compared with shopping in a High Street store.

7. Explain the terms Intranet and Extranet. Why might an organisation choose to have an Intranet?

8. Describe four facilities provided by an e-mail package such as Outlook Express.

9. Describe four advantages of e-mail over ordinary mail.

10. (a) What type of software do you need to surf the world wide web?

    (b) Describe briefly three advantages to a company of having its own web site.

CHAPTER 1.5 Computers at Work

Computers or people?

Computers are an indispensable part of our daily lives. There are many reasons why this is so:

- Computers can calculate millions of times faster than humans
- Computers never get tired or need a rest
- Computers can do jobs that it would be dangerous for a human to do
- Computers can store large amounts of information in a very small space
- Computers can find information quickly
- Computers never lose or misplace information

However, no computer has come up with a play or book worth reading, conjured up a new recipe for something worth eating, or given comfort, sympathy or understanding to someone in distress. Computers can aid people in these tasks, but they can never replace them.

In this chapter we'll look at some of the ways in which computers are used in organisations such as businesses, industry, hospitals and schools. We'll start by looking at some large-scale applications.

Business

Business Administration Systems

Computers are used in businesses for keeping customer records, recording orders, printing invoices, keeping accounts, calculating payroll and managing stock, to name just a few applications.

Airline booking systems

Using a network of computers, airlines are able to instantly record a booking on any flight. Using a computerised booking system it is impossible to sell the same seat twice, even though thousands of people all over the world may be booking flights with a particular airline at any one time.

Online banking

Most banks now offer some form of online banking. Advantages to the customer include access to their account details at any time without the need to travel to a high street branch. Many people are still concerned about the level of security of these systems and the lack of personal contact if problems arise. The main advantage to the banks is a reduction in the cost of running and staffing branches which can lead to job losses.

Insurance claims processing

The Insurance industry, like many other organisations, has to maintain huge databases of customers and their insurance policies. When a customer makes a claim, the computer can quickly find the customer's record and determine the conditions under which payment will be made and, if so, how much. In addition, the computer can be used to automatically send renewal notices to customers when the policy is about to run out.

Government

Many government-run organisations rely heavily on computers to process millions of records every month. Some of these are listed below.

Census

Every few years the government takes a **census** to determine how many people live in the UK, as well as various statistics on age, ethnic origin and income. These census records are held on computer and can be analysed to ensure that the right number of schools, hospitals and other facilities are made available in different areas of the country.

Electronic voting

A voting register of all adults eligible to vote is regularly updated and held on computer. Electronic voting, either at a polling booth or from home via a computer or telephone, has been trialled in local elections and is likely to become widespread.

Vehicle registration

The DVLC computers at Swansea keep a record of every licensed vehicle in the UK, including the make of car, registration number and registered owner.

Revenue collection

The Inland Revenue keeps records of every tax payer, and processes their income tax returns. It is now possible to fill in an income tax return online rather than using a paper form.

Healthcare

Patient records systems

Doctors' surgeries are computerised with more patient record systems being introduced. Appointment booking systems are computerised and doctors automatically print out prescriptions from their PCs.

Ambulance control systems

Many ambulance services are computerised. The objectives of such a system include

- ❶   Call-taking, accepting and verifying incident details
- ❶   Determining which ambulance to send
- ❶   Communicating details of an incident to the chosen ambulance
- ❶   Positioning suitably equipped and staffed vehicles in locations where they are most likely to be needed, so minimising response times to calls

Diagnostic tools and instruments

Computerised diagnostic tools include equipment to take scans or analyse blood, urine and tissue samples. Specialised equipment is also used to monitor vital signs such as heart rate and temperature. Computerised devices such as pacemakers and prostheses (artificial limbs) have enabled tens of thousands of people to live longer and fuller lives.

Specialist surgical equipment

Computers are now used to assist surgeons carrying out surgical operations. Special equipment can provide three-dimensional vision and eliminate hand tremor by scaling down the range of motion.

Education

Student registration and timetabling systems

Computers are widely used in schools and colleges to keep student records. In some schools, students register their presence each day by swiping a magnetic card through a machine.

School timetabling systems are commonly used to work out the timetable for each individual class or pupil.

Computer-based training (CBT)

Software packages which enable students to learn any subject at their computer screens are widely available. They are used not only in schools but also in organisations to teach anything from a foreign language to how to advise a customer on the correct mortgage.

Homework using the Internet

The Internet is an excellent resource to help students complete homework. Some schools and colleges use e-mail to set and collect homework.

Distance learning

ICT is spreading rapidly in education from Primary schools right through to Universities. With ICT firmly on the National Curriculum, students now gain invaluable experience of ICT in the classroom before they embark on a career.

Spending on ICT facilities in educational establishments has increased dramatically over the last decade, and a majority of schools and colleges have dedicated ICT staff and management. Most schools and colleges operate their computers on a network basis so students can access their files and materials from any terminal in their institution. Some can gain access remotely, e.g. from home, which is especially useful to those who cannot attend school for whatever reason.

Teleworking

This term means replacing the journey to work that many people make each day with the use of telecommunications and computers. When teleworking first became acceptable business practice, it was often programmers who had no daily face-to-face contact with other people who became teleworkers. Now, more and more organisations, particularly large ones, are allowing employees to spend time out of the office working from home, for some or all of their weekly hours. The number of teleworkers in Europe is expected to grow from 10 million in 2000 to more than 28.8 million in 2005, according to researcher IDC.

The benefits to employees of teleworking include:

- reduced cost of travelling
- long commuting journeys avoided
- opportunity to work in the comfort of their own home environment
- increased productivity
- greater ability to focus on one task
- flexible schedules
- reduced company space requirements
- easier childcare arrangements

The drawbacks include:

- lack of personal contact with fellow workers
- lack of teamwork and participation with shared projects
- home distractions may interfere with work
- lack of benefits given to other employees who attend the office, e.g. medical plans, pensions and bonuses

Ergonomics

As people spend more and more time using computers it is essential to create an **ergonomic** working environment. Ergonomics refers to design and functionality and encompasses a range of factors:

- **Lighting**. The room should be well lit. Computers should neither face windows nor back onto a window so that the users have to sit with the sun in their eyes. Adjustable blinds should be provided.

- **Ventilation**. The room should have opening windows to allow free circulation of air and to prevent overheating.

- **Furniture**. Chairs should be of adjustable height, with a backrest which tilts to support the user at work and at rest, and should swivel on a five-point base. It should be at the correct height relative to a keyboard on the desk.

- **Accessories**. Document holders, mouse mats, paper trays, foot rests etc. should be provided where appropriate.

- **Hardware**. The screen should tilt and swivel and be flicker-free. Ideally it should be situated so that it avoids reflecting light. A removable monitor filter can be useful to prevent glare. The keyboard should be separately attached.

All computer users should be encouraged to take frequent breaks away from the computer.

Health issues

Computers can be held responsible for many health problems, from eyestrain to wrist injuries and back problems.

- **Repetitive Strain Injury** (RSI). This is the collective name for a variety of disorders affecting the neck, shoulders and upper limbs. It can result in numbness or tingling in the arms and hands, aching and stiffness in the arms, neck and shoulders, and an inability to lift or grip objects. The Health and Safety Executive say that more than 100,000 workers suffer from RSI.

- **Eyestrain**. Computer users are prone to eyestrain from spending long hours in front of a screen. Many computer users prefer a dim light to achieve better screen contrast, but this makes it difficult to read documents on the desk. A small spotlight focused on the desktop can be helpful. There is no evidence that computer use causes permanent damage to the eyes but glare, improper lighting, improperly corrected vision (through not wearing the correct prescription glasses), poor work practices and poorly designed workstations all contribute to temporary eyestrain. Users should be allowed regular breaks away from the screen.

- **Back problems**. Poor seating and bad posture whilst sitting at a computer screen can cause back problems.

Safety precautions

All cables should be safely secured and power points not overloaded. Working surfaces should be clean and tidy.

The environment

There are a number of measures that computer users can take to help the environment:

- recycle printer toner cartridges
- recycle printer paper
- use systems that use less power while inactive
- CD-ROM materials, electronic documents and on-screen help all reduce the need for printed materials

Exercises

1. Describe briefly five situations when you may use or encounter computers other than your own PC, in everyday life.

2. Describe briefly three large-scale uses of computers by government, describing in each case what data is held and how it may be used.

3. Give three advantages and three disadvantages of computer-based training in a school or company.

4. Describe briefly three health hazards associated with working long hours at a computer. In each case, describe one method of minimising the hazard.

5. (a) Describe briefly three ways in which users can minimise the detrimental effects of computers on the environment.

   (b) Describe three ways in which computers could be said to be contributing positively towards preserving the environment.

6. What is meant by **teleworking**? Name two advantages to:

   (a) the employer

   (b) the employee

Legal Issues and Security

Copyright

Computer software is **copyright** material – that means it is protected in the UK by the Copyright, Designs and Patents Act 1988. It is owned by the software producer and it is illegal to make unauthorised copies.

When you buy software it is often supplied in a sealed package (e.g. CD ROM case) on which the terms and conditions of sale are printed. This is called the software **licence** and when the user opens the package they are agreeing to abide by the licence terms (this is often referred to as the End User Licence Agreement). The CD or package will have a unique Product ID number which you may need to type in when installing the software. Once installed, you can see the Product ID number by clicking on the **Help** menu and selecting an option such as, for example, **About Microsoft Word**.

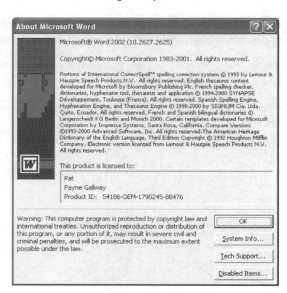

Software licences usually permit the user to use one copy on any single computer. It is considered to be in use if it is loaded into either the computer's temporary memory (RAM) or onto the hard disk drive. With network licences the software is often loaded onto the file server and the licence specifies how many users on the network can access it at any one time.

It is illegal to make copies of the software, except for backup purposes, so you are breaking the law if you copy some software from a friend onto removable media such as floppy disk, CD or Zip disk to use on your own computer.

Some software is classed as **shareware**. This can be downloaded from the Internet for evaluation. If you like the program you pay a fee and register with the manufacturer. Most programs of this type allow you to use them a limited number of times and then cease to load correctly when the evaluation period expires.

Freeware programs can be downloaded from the Internet and used for no cost.

Files downloaded from the Internet containing text, graphics, audio or video clips may also be copyright. It is illegal to use such material in your own publications without the consent of the author or creator.

Personal privacy

The **right to privacy** is a fundamental human right and one that we take for granted. Most of us, for instance, would not want our medical records freely circulated, and many people are sensitive about revealing their age, religious beliefs, family circumstances or academic qualifications. In the UK even the use of name and address files for mail shots is often felt to be an invasion of privacy.

With the advent of large computerised databases it became quite feasible for sensitive personal information to be stored without the individual's knowledge and accessed by, say, a prospective employer, credit card company or insurance company to assess somebody's suitability for employment, credit or insurance.

Case study: James Wiggins – a true story

In the US, James Russell Wiggins applied for and got a $70,000 post with a company in Washington. A routine pre-employment background check, however, revealed that he had been convicted of possessing cocaine, and he was fired the next day, not only because he had a criminal record but because he had concealed this fact when applying for the job. Wiggins was shocked – he had never had a criminal record, and it turned out that the credit bureau hired to make the investigation had retrieved the record for a James Ray Wiggins by mistake, even though they had different birthdates, addresses, middle names and social security numbers. Even after this was discovered, however, Wiggins didn't get his job back.

If the pre-employment check had been made before Wiggins was offered the job, he would not have been offered it and no reason would have been given. The information would have remained on his file, virtually ensuring that he would never get a decent job – without ever knowing the reason why.

The Data Protection Act

The **Data Protection Act** 1998 came into force on 1 March 2000. It sets rules for processing information about people and applies to paper records as well as those held on computers. It is intended to protect the privacy of individuals.

The Data Protection Principles

Anyone holding personal data must comply with the eight enforceable principles of good practice. They say that data must be:

- Fairly and lawfully processed
- Obtained only for specific purposes
- Adequate, relevant and not excessive
- Accurate and up-to-date
- Not kept longer than necessary
- Processed in accordance with the data subject's rights
- Not transferred to other countries without adequate protection
- Secure and safe from others who don't have rights to it e.g. other employees and hackers

Any organisation holding personal data about people (for example employees or customers) must register with the Data Protection Registrar. They have to state what data is being held, the sources and purposes of the data and the types of organisations to whom the data may be disclosed.

As an individual you are entitled, on making a written request to a data user, to be supplied with a copy of any personal data held about yourself. The data user may charge a fee of up to £10 for each register entry for supplying this information but in some cases it is supplied free.

Usually the request must be responded to within 40 days. If not, you are entitled to complain to the Registrar or apply to the courts for correction or deletion of the data.

With some exceptions, data cannot be held about you without your consent.

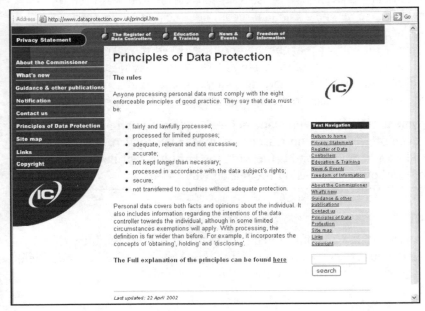

For more information on Data Protection visit the following web site:
www.dataprotection.gov.uk

Data security

One of the legal requirements of the Data Protection Act is that data about individuals must be kept secure. This means that it must be properly protected from unauthorised view or loss. Moreover, the data held on a computer system can be one of the most valuable assets of a company. Security controls must be put in place to protect it from damage and unauthorised access.

To deal with security risks, most organisations have an information security policy. A typical security policy will cover:

- Administrative controls such as careful screening of prospective employees and disciplinary procedures in the event of security breaches
- Backup procedures
- Control of access to data by means of smart cards, ID badges, sign-in/sign-out registers
- Protection against fire and flood
- Access controls to computer systems and data by means of user IDs, passwords and access rights
- Procedures for reporting security incidents
- Training to make staff members aware of their responsibilities

Backup procedures

Backing up data involves copying it to a removable storage device such as magnetic tape, CD-ROM, Zip drive etc. A backup of all data is typically made on a daily basis, or more frequently, depending on the nature and importance of the data. The backup media must be clearly labelled and should be stored in a fire-proof safe, or better still on a different site, so that should a disaster or emergency occur, the backup media will be safe.

Access controls

Most networks require a user to log on with a **user-id** and **password** before they can gain access to the computer system. The user-id is normally assigned to you, and is open to view. The password is secret and does not appear on the screen when you type it in – the letters may be replaced by asterisks as you type. You can change your password whenever you like.

If you are authorised to access particularly sensitive data which only certain people are allowed to view, you may need to enter a second password. For example, on a company database the Accounts clerks may be able to view customer records but they may not be allowed access to personal data about colleagues. These **access rights** are used to protect the privacy of individuals and the security of confidential data.

In order to be completely secure there are some basic rules you should follow when using a password:

- ❶ Never write the password down – commit it to memory
- ❶ Never tell your password to another person
- ❶ Do not use an obvious word or name as a password – a combination of at least 6 letters and numbers is best
- ❶ Change your password regularly

Theft

The theft of a laptop computer, PDA or mobile phone can have disastrous consequences for the owner if they have not backed up their data. Confidential files, lists of phone numbers which could be misused, contact details or months of work can be lost if they are not properly protected and backed up.

Computer viruses

Viruses are generally developed with a definite intention to cause damage to computer files or, at the very least, cause inconvenience and annoyance to computer users. Precautions to avoid your PC being infected with a virus include the following:

- ❶ **Virus checkers** need to be installed on all computer systems so that they automatically check for any infected data when the computer is started up. Manual checkers can also be used to check for viruses on floppy disks.
- ❶ You should not share or lend floppy disks that could introduce viruses into your system.
- ❶ Care should be taken when downloading files from the Internet. The proliferation of viruses over recent years is due in part to e-mail communication. Never open an unrecognised e-mail message or an e-mail attachment from someone that you don't recognise – it could well introduce a virus to your system.

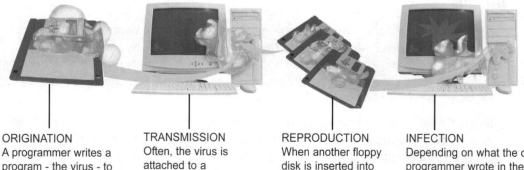

ORIGINATION
A programmer writes a program - the virus - to cause mischief or destruction. The virus is capable of reproducing itself.

TRANSMISSION
Often, the virus is attached to a normal program. It then copies itself to other software on the hard disk.

REPRODUCTION
When another floppy disk is inserted into the computer's disk drive, the virus copies itself on to the floppy disk.

INFECTION
Depending on what the original programmer wrote in the virus program, a virus may dsiplay messages, use up all the computer's memory, destroy data files or cause serious damage.

As approximately 300 new viruses are unleashed each month it is a good idea to install a virus checker that provides an online update service. You will automatically receive a message to update which can be done online.

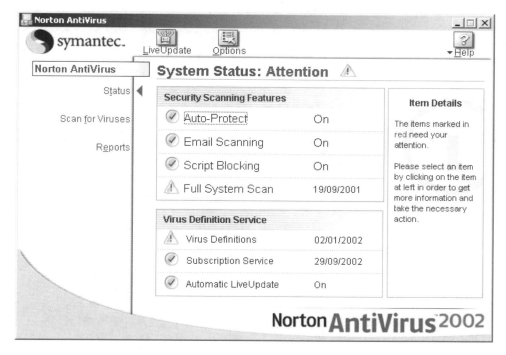

The virus checker software should be capable of not only detecting the virus, but also of removing it from the infected file (this called **disinfecting** the file).

Exercises

1. What is meant by the terms shareware and freeware? Can you use such software without paying, on your computer?

2. Before using a photograph that you have downloaded from the Internet in a publication of your own, what should you do?

3. (a) What is the name of the Act that protects the privacy of personal data held on a computer?

   (b) List four provisions of this Act.

4. What rights do you have as an individual, regarding the holding of personal data about yourself on a computer?

5. (a) What is a computer virus?

   (b) Name three measures you can take to minimise the possibility of your computer being infected with a virus.

Index — Concepts of Information Technology

Module 2
Using the Computer and Managing Files

In this module you will learn to become competent in using the common functions of a personal computer and its operating system. You will learn how to:

- adjust main settings
- use the built-in help features and deal with a non-responding application
- operate effectively within the desktop environment and work with desktop icons and windows
- manage and organise files and directories/folders
- duplicate, move and delete files and directories/folders, and compress and extract files
- use virus-scanning software
- use simple editing tools and print management facilities available within the operating system

Module 2   Table of Contents

The Desktop

First steps

This module will give you invaluable skills in using your computer's **operating system** – in this case, **MS Windows**. The version of Windows used here is Windows XP, but you will find that other versions of Windows work in much the same way. The things you will learn in this module will help you to organise all the work you do using applications such as word processing and spreadsheets.

It will also help you to 'trouble shoot' and know what to do when something unexpected happens. Hopefully it will take a lot of the bafflement and frustration out of using your computer!

Switching on

◉ Check that the floppy disk drive is empty.

◉ Press the power switch on the front of the system unit. Also remember to switch on the screen and the printer.

◉ If you are working on a network you will probably be asked to enter a user ID and password. Do that now. For security reasons, the password will not be displayed on the screen.

Wait for the screen to stop changing. It should end up with some small symbols (called icons) and a coloured background – this is called your **desktop**.

Office toolbar

Icons

Taskbar

Depending on how your computer has been set up you may see a different background and you may not see the Office toolbar – this provides shortcuts to some programs.

Let's look more closely at the desktop.

Icons

Desktop icons come in a variety of different forms. Here are some of the common ones:

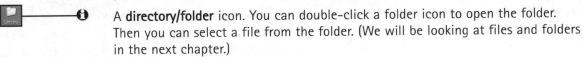   A **directory/folder** icon. You can double-click a folder icon to open the folder. Then you can select a file from the folder. (We will be looking at files and folders in the next chapter.)

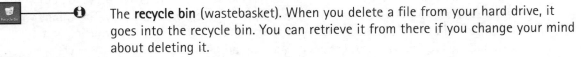   A **file** icon. Double-click a file icon to open the file in the appropriate application – in this case, Word.

   An **application** icon. You can double-click on an application icon to open the application.

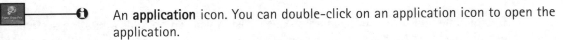   The **recycle bin** (wastebasket). When you delete a file from your hard drive, it goes into the recycle bin. You can retrieve it from there if you change your mind about deleting it.

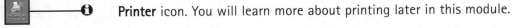   **Printer** icon. You will learn more about printing later in this module.

You will have a completely different selection of icons on your desktop, and maybe a different background as well. Later on in Chapter 2.5 you will learn how to select a different background for your desktop.

Task bar

The Task bar at the bottom of the screen shows application programs that are currently open. It also has icons on it which you can click to return to the desktop if it is not currently visible, launch Internet Explorer and view the current date and time.

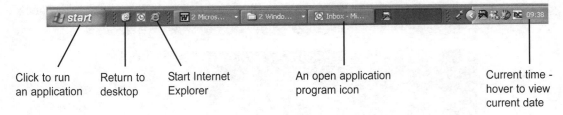

| Click to run an application | Return to desktop | Start Internet Explorer | An open application program icon | Current time - hover to view current date |

   ○   Hover the mouse over any icon on the Task bar. A **Tool tip** appears telling you its function.

Using the mouse

This is the left button, and is the one most often used. When you are asked to click the mouse button, press this button once.

This is the right button, and is used to bring up a pop-up menu in Windows, so called because the menu pops up from nowhere.

Depending on where the mouse pointer is on the screen, or what the computer is doing, a different icon appears. Here are some examples:

This is the general pointer and means the computer is ready for you to do something.

The hour-glass shows the computer is busy, maybe loading a program, and you should wait until the normal pointer appears before you do anything

When the pointer changes to a two-headed arrow you can re-size a window.

Mouse clicks

There are basically three different ways of clicking a mouse button that you will be using. You will also need to drag to select or move text or objects.

- ❶ **Single-click**. When you are told to 'click', this means **Click the left button once**. Clicking once selects an item. Try clicking on one of the desktop icons. It changes colour but nothing else happens.

- ❶ **Double-click**. Generally speaking, clicking selects an item, and double-clicking activates it - but there are plenty of exceptions to this rule. Try double-clicking the My Computer icon, for example, to open the **My Computer** window. You can leave this window open on the desktop for now.

- ❶ **Right-click**. When you are told to right-click, click the right-hand button once. This opens a pop-up menu showing various things that can be done. Try this by right-clicking on the desktop. Click away from the pop-up menu to close it again.

- ❶ **Drag**. Click on an item and hold down the left mouse button while you drag the mouse. The selected item will move.

- ◐ Try moving a desktop icon by dragging it.

Tip:

If the icon won't move, right-click the Desktop and select **Arrange icons By**. Make sure **Auto Arrange** is not selected.

The Start button

The **Start** button at the bottom left of the screen is used to select an application to run or a task that you want to do – including shutting down your computer!

We'll open a games application now.

- ● Click the **Start** button.

- ● On the menu that appears, click **Programs**.

- ● On the submenu, select **Games**. On the next menu, select **Solitaire**.

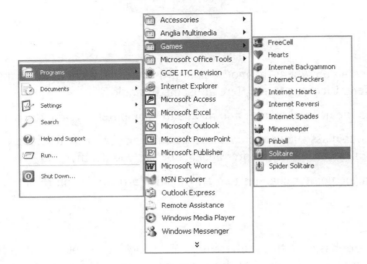

Tip:
If your start menu looks different, right-click the **Start** button and click **Properties**. Click the **Start Menu** tab and select the **Classic Start menu** option.

The Solitaire window opens.

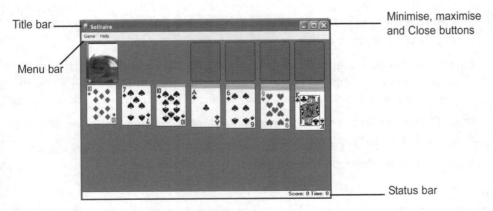

Title bar

Menu bar

Minimise, maximise and Close buttons

Status bar

Ooh! I can put that Ace up!

The parts of a window

If you can tear yourself away from the game, or can't figure out how to play, we'll look now at the parts of a window.

You should have two windows open on the desktop – the **My Computer** window and the **Solitaire** window. You'll notice that each of them has the following parts in common:

❶   A **Title bar** showing the name of the program. Click in the title bar of each window in turn to bring it to the foreground.

❶   A **Menu bar** that has labels that when clicked produce dropdown menus with options to choose from.

❶   A **Status bar** which provides information about the current state of what you are viewing in the window.

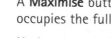

❶   A **Minimise** button. Click this button once in the Solitaire window. The window disappears, but the application is still open. Look in the Task bar and you will see an icon named **Solitaire**. Click it to restore the window to the desktop.

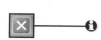

❶   A **Maximise** button. Click this once in the Solitaire window. The window now occupies the full screen.

❶   Notice that the **Maximise** button has now changed to a **Restore Down** button. Click this once now to restore the window to its original size.

❶   A **Close** button. You would click this once to close the window. Don't do this now. If you do close one of the two open windows, open it up again!

❶   Horizontal and vertical scroll bars that can be moved to allow you to see all parts of the window.

Moving and resizing a window

Either click the icons on the task bar or click the Title bar of a window to switch between open windows. You can move a window around on the screen by dragging its Title bar.

To change the size of a window, move the cursor over one of the window borders so that it changes to a double-headed arrow. Then drag one way or the other to make the window bigger or smaller.

▶   Try making the **My Computer** window smaller so that scroll bars appear.

You can drag a scroll bar to see parts of the window that are hidden from view.

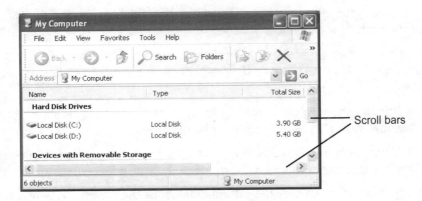

Scroll bars

Notice that this window also has a Toolbar with buttons which you can click.

◉ Try arranging the windows on the desktop so that they don't overlap. A quick way to do this is to right-click in the Task bar and from the pop-up menu, select **Tile Windows Horizontally** or **Tile Windows Vertically**.

◉   Close both the open windows when you have finished practising.

Switching off your computer

Before you switch off your computer you must close any programs that are open. You should then close your computer down in the recommended way. If you don't do this and just switch off, your computer will not restart normally next time.

◉   When you have closed all your programs you should see only the Windows desktop on the screen.

◉   In the bottom left-hand corner of your screen, click **Start**.

◉   Click **Shut Down**.

◉   In the box that appears check that the **Shut down** option is displayed and click **OK**.

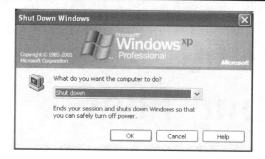

○ Wait for the screen to go black, or for a message to say that it is safe to turn off your computer and then switch off the computer.

Tip:
With Windows 2000 or later versions, the PC switches itself off.

Restarting your computer

Instead of closing down your computer you can choose to restart it. You may want to do this if you have loaded some new software and the instructions tell you to restart Windows.

○ When you reach the dialogue box shown above, click the down-arrow and select **Restart** from the dropdown list.

Exercises

1. Switch on your computer and look at the Windows desktop. Write down the answers to the following questions on a sheet of paper.

    (a) Do you have to enter a Windows username and password?

    (b) What are icons?

    (c) Write down the names of all the icons you can see.

    (d) What is the recycle bin icon used for?

    (e) Where would you find the current date and time on your Windows desktop?

    (f) What does it mean when you see an hour-glass on the screen?

    (g) Describe how you would open the Solitaire game.

2. Open the **My Computer** window and the **Solitaire** game and answer the following questions:

    (a) Describe the purpose of the window **Minimise** and **Maximise** buttons.

    (b) Describe how you would resize a window.

    (c) Draw a rough sketch of a screen with two windows tiled vertically.

3. Why shouldn't you just switch off your computer without closing down correctly?

4. How would you restart your computer?

5. Give one example of when you might need to restart your computer.

Creating and Printing Files

In this chapter we'll open some of the applications that you will learn about in other modules, and save some sample files of different types in a folder.

A text editing application

First we will create a short document and save it.

🔘 From the **Start** menu select **Programs, Accessories, Wordpad.**

> **Tip:**
> This is a short way used in this book of saying 'Click **Start**. From the submenu select **Programs**. From the next submenu select **Accessories**. From the next submenu select **Wordpad**.'

Wordpad is a simple text editor that is supplied free with Windows.

🔘 Type a short sentence – you can be more imaginative if you like!

This is a test document created in Wordpad.

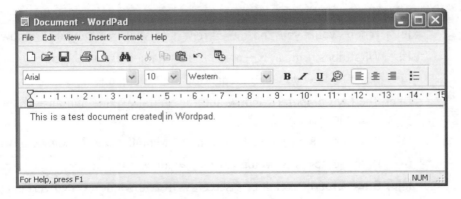

🔘 From the **File** menu, select **Save**.

A window will open, probably showing the default **My Documents** folder in the **Save in**: box. If it shows something different, you can either ask for help from your teacher or just save it in the folder shown. Later, you will learn how to move it.

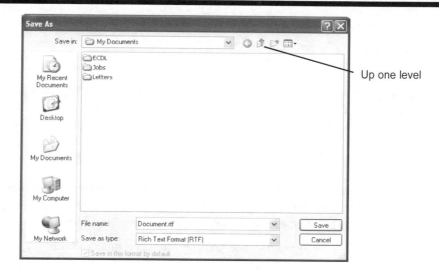

Up one level

○ In the **File name** box type the name **Wordpad-Test**.

Notice that by default, it will be saved as a type of file called Rich Text Format. A full stop followed by the three letters RTF will be added to the end of your file name. These letters are known as the file **extension**.

○ Click **Save**. The window will close automatically.

 ○ Close **Wordpad** by clicking the **Close** icon or by selecting **File, Exit**.

Opening an existing file

Now practise re-opening Wordpad and opening the new file you created.

○ Open Microsoft Wordpad.

○ Select **File, Open**.

The Open dialogue box will be displayed.

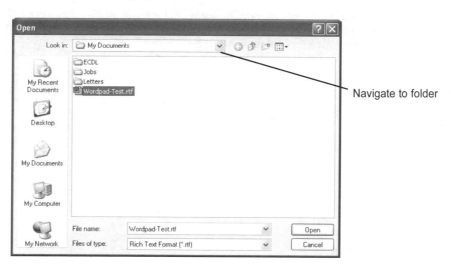

Navigate to folder

◉   Navigate to the correct file(s), select the files(s).

◉   Click **Open**.

> **Tip:**
> If you wanted to open more than one file, you can hold down the **Shift** key while you select each file.

File types

Windows recognises many different file types. The file type depends on which application the file was created in. Here are some examples of common file types, each identified by the three-character **extension** which forms part of the file name.

.doc	A word-processed file produced in MS Word
.xls	A spreadsheet produced in MS Excel
.mdb	A database created in MS Access
.ppt	A presentation file created in MS PowerPoint
.bmp	A bitmapped graphic created in a graphics package
.jpg, .gif, .tif	Different types of graphics file
.mp3, .mid, .wav	An audio file
.avi, .mpeg, .mov	A video file
.txt	A plain text file
.zip	A compressed file
.htm	A web page file
.tmp	A temporary file

> **Tip:**
> In Chapter 2.3 you will learn how to rename a file. However, you have to be careful not to change the extension because the software will not recognise the file type and will not know how to handle your file.

Creating Word documents

Next we'll create three very short documents using Word. We need some files of different types so that we can practise moving them, copying them, renaming them and so on in the next chapter!

● Open **Word**. You can do this by clicking the **Word** icon in the Office toolbar, if you have one. Alternatively, click the **Start** button and select **Programs, Microsoft Word**.

● Type a short invitation to your friend Sharon.

> Dear Sharon
>
> We're having a party on Friday 13th. Hope you can come!

● From the **File** menu select **Save**. Save the document in the same folder as before, naming it **Sharon**.

● Now edit the letter by changing the name **Sharon** to **Robert**.

● This time, you don't want to select **Save** from the **File** menu because that would simply overwrite the contents of the original file, leaving you with a letter to Robert with the file name **Sharon**. Instead, select **Save As**.

● Type the new file name **Robert**.

● Edit the letter once more, to send an invitation to **Kim**.

● Save this file as **Kim**.

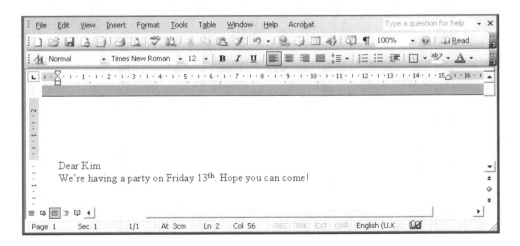

Creating some spreadsheet files

Now we'll create some spreadsheet files.

○ Open **Microsoft Excel**. This program is used to hold numerical information and you'll learn all about it in Module 4. For now, we'll just enter a single number in cell A1.

○ In cell A1 enter the number **1**. Press **Enter**.

○ Save the spreadsheet as **SS1**.

○ Create 3 more spreadsheets, naming them **SS2**, **SS3** and **SS4**. You can do this in the same way as you created the three Word documents.

 ○ Close Excel by clicking the **Close** icon or by selecting **File**, **Exit**.

Printing a file

If you have not closed down Microsoft Word, you should see the name of the last document that you saved in the Task bar.

○ Click the file name in the Task bar and the document will open.

○ From the **File** menu select **Print**.

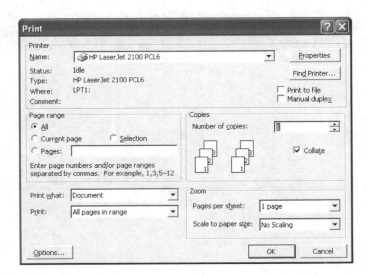

The print dialogue box allows you to choose many options including which printer you want to use (if you are working on a network), which page you want to print (for longer documents) and how many copies you would like.

O   Check that there is some paper in the printer.

O   Make sure that only one copy is selected and click **OK**.

Your letter will print out.

The desktop print manager

When you send a document to the printer to be printed, a printer icon appears in the **System Tray** at the right-hand end of the Task bar.

You can right-click on this icon to view the print job's progress. The following window will be displayed:

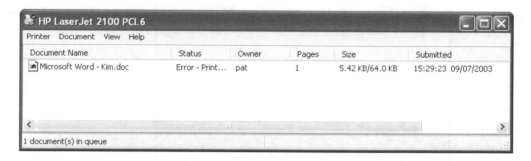

Pausing, restarting or deleting a print job

In the screenshot for the print job, the status is given as Error. (In this case it was because the printer was not switched on.)

You can pause, restart or cancel a print job by clicking the file name. A pop-up menu appears:

Shutting down a non-responding application

From time to time, just when you think things are going really well and that you are getting to grips with using a PC, everything suddenly grinds to a halt and it refuses to respond. Your application has 'crashed'!

If your screen locks up so that you cannot use the keyboard or mouse, you can try to find out which program is causing the problem.

○   Press **Ctrl-Alt-Del** on the keyboard (all at the same time). In the window that appears click **Task Manager**.

All the applications currently running in your computer will be listed. One of them will probably show a status of **Not Responding**. This will be the offending program.

○   Click the name of the program and click **End Task** to close it.

This should close down the faulty program and allow you to carry on working. If it doesn't, follow the **Shut Down** procedure – this will close your PC down safely.

Unfortunately, either way you will lose anything you have been working on in the application – for example, all the changes to a document since you last saved it. The only lesson to be learned is to save your work every few minutes. Everything that you have saved to a floppy disk or hard disk is safe.

Tip:
A quick way to save a document you are currently working on is to press **Ctrl-S** (**Ctrl** and **S** together) on the keyboard. Alternatively, click the **Save** icon.

○   Close Microsoft Word.

Exercises

1. Open a new WordPad document.

2. Enter the following text:

   Different file types include the following:

3. Move to a blank line by pressing **Enter** and type in the names of as many common file types as possible. Leave a couple of spaces between each one.

4. Save this document as **File types.rtf** in your **My Documents** folder.

5. Open a new Microsoft Word document.

6. In the document describe how you would access the desktop print manager and explain what it does.

7. Save this document as **Print Manager.doc** in your **My Documents** folder.

8. Click on your document **File types.rtf** in the Task bar and print it out.

9. Return to **Print Manager.doc** and print that too.

10. Add some more text to the document **Print Manager.doc**. This should explain how to close a non-responding application.

11. Save the document with the name **Useful tips.doc** and print out a copy.

12. Close the file **Filetypes.rtf** and close WordPad.

13. Close **Print Manager.doc** and **Useful tips.doc** and close Word.

CHAPTER

2.3 Folders and Files

Disk drives on your computer

You probably have several disk drives on your computer. Windows assigns a letter to each of them. The floppy drive is usually A:, the hard drive C:, the zip drive (if you have one) is probably D:, the CD drive E: and so on. On a network the hard drive is usually divided or 'partitioned' into several 'logical drives' called, for example, F:, G:, H: etc.

You can see what drives your computer has, and how much free space there is on each disk.

O   Go to the Desktop. You can do this by clicking the Desktop icon next to the **Start** button at the bottom left of the screen, or by right-clicking in the Task bar and selecting **Show the Desktop**.

O   Double-click the **My Computer** icon. You should see a window similar to the one below:

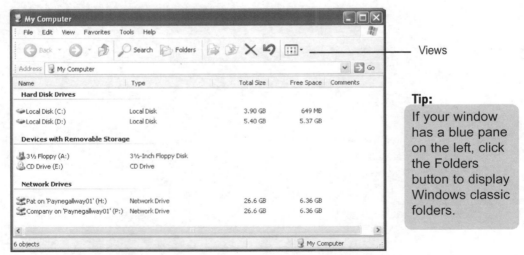

Views

Tip:
If your window has a blue pane on the left, click the Folders button to display Windows classic folders.

The screenshot shows two hard disk drives, C: and D:. Actually there is only one physical drive, but for convenience it has been divided into two partitions. The same has been done on the network drive. What drives do you have on your computer?

Your screen may still look different. You can change the appearance of the window by clicking the **Views** button, and selecting one of the other options.

Directories/folders

All the documents you create on your PC are referred to as **files**. These files have to be given names (you can use up to 255 characters) and it is a good idea to use meaningful file names so that you can easily find a particular file later on.

As you use your computer more and more you will have lots of files stored on your hard drive (**C:**). You will need to keep your work organised so that you can go to it quickly.

Files are organised by saving them into **folders** that are also given names. These folders can contain subfolders. One very important folder that is set up automatically for you is **My Documents**. This is where Windows expects you to create your own subfolders to store your work.

Tip:

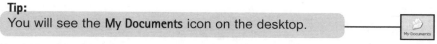

You will see the **My Documents** icon on the desktop.

Here is an example of a folder structure within **My Documents**:

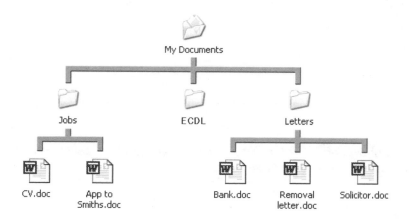

The location of files is specified by their **pathname**. For example in the diagram above, the pathname to the word-processed file **Removal letter** would be as follows:

C:\My Documents\Letters\Removal letter.doc

❍   Double-click the **C:** drive icon.

You will now see a window displaying the folders on the C: drive. (Your window will have different folders.)

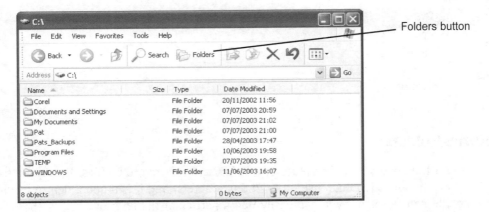

Folders button

○ Click the **Folders** button if it is not already selected. This shows you a more detailed view.

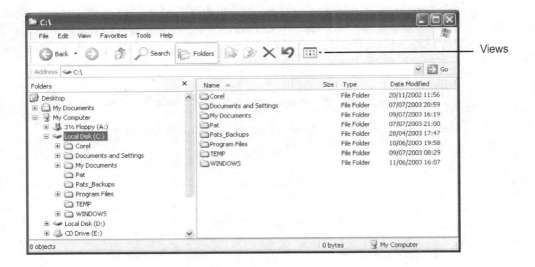

Views

Tip:
The view shown above is the **Details** view. Click the **Views** button to change to this view if your screen looks different.

Creating a new folder

We will set up the folders and subfolders shown on the previous page.

○ Double-click on **My Documents**. The folder opens.

○ From the **File** menu, select **New**. Then select **Folder**.

○ Type the name **Jobs** as the **New Folder** name.

- Click the **Back** button to go back to the **My Documents** folder.
- Create the other two folders **ECDL** and **Letters** in the same way.
- Click the **ECDL** folder and create the two subfolders **Module1** and **Module2**.

Back ——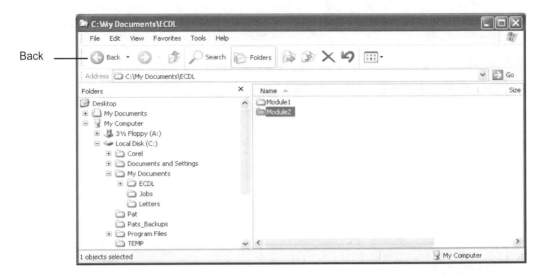

Tip:
Right-clicking on a folder and selecting **Properties** will tell you the total size of the folder and the number of subfolders and files it contains.

Navigating to a file or folder

- In the left-hand pane, click **My Documents**. Now you should see all the subfolders you created, and all the files you saved in **My Documents**.

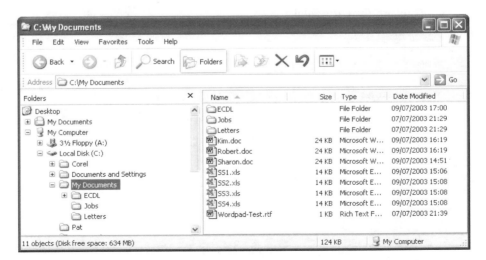

Notice that you can now see the hierarchy of folders and files: when you clicked **My Documents**, the little + sign beside it in the left-hand window changed to a – sign. The + sign indicates that there are subfolders within this folder, which can be viewed by clicking to expand the structure.

This needs practice. For example, if you click the + sign beside the **ECDL** folder, you will see it expanded in the left-hand window, but it is not the selected folder so the right-hand pane will still show the contents of **My Documents**, the selected folder.

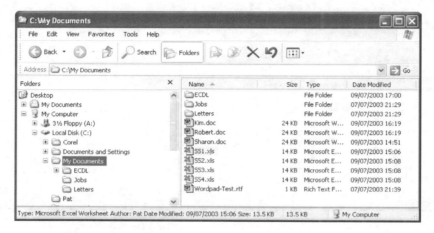

 Practise clicking the + and – signs beside various folders, and selecting folders and subfolders, until you are clear about how the system works. Leave your screen looking like the one above for the next task.

Renaming a file

You can rename any file or folder.

 Right-click on **Kim.doc**. Then select **Rename**.

A pop-up window will appear:

○ Change the file name to **Tom.doc** by typing the new name over the old one and pressing **Enter**. If you do not enter **.doc** correctly, you will be warned that changing the extension may make the file unusable. Be sure to get it right!

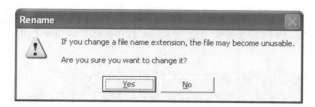

Changing file status

○ Right-click on **Robert.doc**. Then select **Properties**.

The Properties window appears and you can change the file status to **Read-only** if you don't want to accidentally change the file. Sometimes you may find that a file has accidentally been set to Read-only, and you can reset it to Read/Write (i.e. not Read-only) in this window.

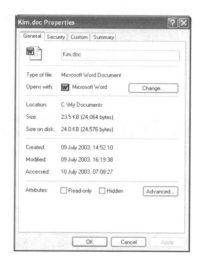

Tip:
When a file is set to Read-only, you won't be able to save any changes you make to it if you try and edit it. A message will be displayed:

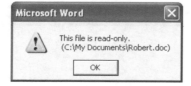

Sorting files

You can change the order in which files are displayed in the right-hand window by clicking in the bar on **Name**, **Size**, **Type** or **Date Modified** to sort the files and folders in any of these sequences.

○ Click once on **Name**. The files will be sorted in alphabetical order of name, from A-Z.

○ Click again on **Name**. The files will be sorted in sequence from Z-A.

○ Try sorting the files in different sequences, for example, by file type. Leave the files sorted in ascending order of name.

Selecting files and folders

Sometimes you need to reorganise your files, perhaps moving them into different folders. Other times you may want to copy one or more files into a different folder or onto a floppy disk for backup.

Instead of moving them one at a time, you can select all the files you want to move and then move them in one operation.

❶ To select several adjacent files or folders, click the first file name. Then hold down the **Shift** key while you click the last file name you want to select.

❶ To select non-adjacent files, hold down the **Ctrl** key while you select each one.

○ Select all the **.doc** files.

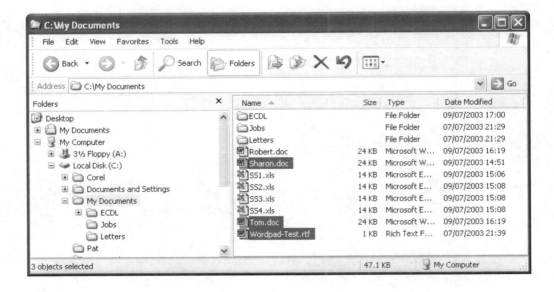

Copying and moving files and folders

You can copy a file to another folder or disk drive by first copying it to the **Clipboard**, and then pasting it to the desired location.

The **Clipboard** is a temporary storage area which will hold the latest file or folder that you cut or copy. The next time you cut or copy something, the previous contents will be overwritten.

We will copy all the Word documents to the **Letters** folder.

O   With the **.doc** files selected, click **Edit**, **Copy**. This copies all these files to the Clipboard.

O   In the left-hand window, click on the folder name **Letters**.

O   Select **Edit**, **Paste**. The files will be copied to the **Letters** folder.

Now there are two copies of each of these files – in **My Documents** and in **Letters**.

Note that folders can be copied in the same way. When you copy a folder, all its contents are copied too. You can copy to another drive such as the A: drive in exactly the same way.

Making backup copies

Copying files for backup purposes is an essential skill for everyone using a computer! Sooner or later some disaster will occur such as your hard disk crashing, your laptop being stolen, or your file being infected with a virus. That's when you will be glad you have a recent copy of your work on a floppy disk safely tucked away in your desk drawer at home.

Deleting files and folders

You can delete the documents from their original location.

O   Click on **My Documents**.

O   Select the **.doc** files again.

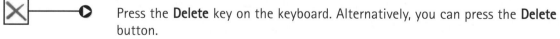   O   Press the **Delete** key on the keyboard. Alternatively, you can press the **Delete** button.

You will see a message:

◉   If you are sure you have selected the correct items, click **Yes**.

Tip:

You could use **Edit**, **Cut** instead of **Edit**, **Copy** when moving files. But you may find it's safer to copy them and then delete the ones you don't want!

The Recycle Bin

So what is this Recycle Bin? It all sounds very environmentally friendly!

When you delete a file or folder, it is not completely deleted – it is moved to a storage area called the **Recycle Bin**. This is very useful because it means that if you deleted the wrong file by mistake, you can retrieve it from the bin!

If you realise your mistake immediately, the easiest way to get your files back is to press the **Undo** button.

Suppose you just want to restore the file **Tom.doc**.

◉   Go to the Desktop by clicking the **Desktop** icon next to the **Start** button in the Task bar. Alternatively, you can right-click in the Task bar and select **Show the Desktop**.

◉   Double-click the **Recycle Bin** on the Desktop.

A window opens showing the contents of the Recycle Bin.

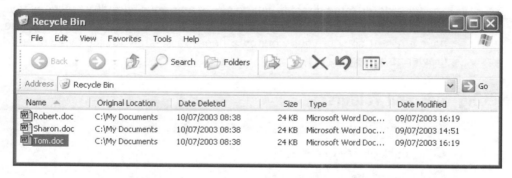

◉   Right-click **Tom.doc** and from the pop-up menu, select **Restore**.

Your file will be restored to the **My Documents** folder.

You can restore deleted folders in the same way.

Emptying the Recycle Bin

The contents of the Recycle Bin take up space on your hard disk and it is a good idea to empty it now and then.

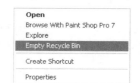

◉ On the Desktop, right-click the **Recycle Bin** and select **Empty Recycle Bin**. You will be asked to confirm your request. Remember there is no getting those files back now!

Drag and Drop

Another way of copying or moving files is to select them and then drag them into the new location.

Be aware of the following rule:

❶ Dragging a file or folder to a new location on the same drive **moves** the file or folder.

❶ Dragging a file or folder to a different drive **copies** the folder.

If you want to use drag and drop to copy a file to a new location on the same drive, hold down **Ctrl** while you drag.

We'll use the Drag and Drop technique to move the spreadsheet files to the folder **Module2**, which is a subfolder of **ECDL**.

◉ Restore the C: window to the desktop. It may be minimised in the Task bar.

◉ Click the + sign next to the ECDL folder name so that its two subfolders are visible.

◉ Click **SS1**, then hold down **Shift** and click **SS4** to select the four spreadsheets.

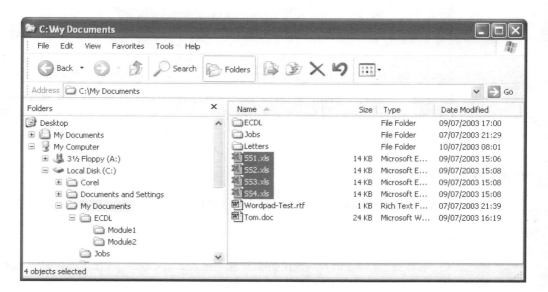

○   Hold down the left mouse button while you drag the files and drop them onto **Module2**.

Navigating within an application

Very often you need to find a file, save a file in a particular folder, create a new folder or delete a file from within an application such as Word.

For example, suppose you want to open the file **Kim.doc** in Word.

○   Open Word. From the **File** menu select **Open**.

The following screen appears:

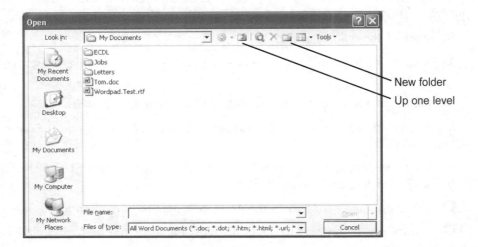

Now suppose you can't remember where the file is saved and you decide to look in **Module2**. You double-click on **ECDL** to display its subfolders. Then double-click **Module2** – no documents! This folder only contains spreadsheets.

You need to navigate backup through the folder structure, and across to **Letters**.

You can do this either by clicking the down-arrow next to the file name in the **Look in**: box, or by clicking the **Up one level** button until you are back at **My Documents**.

Note that you can create a new folder in this window by clicking the **New Folder** button. You can also delete a selected file using either the **Delete** key or the **Delete** button in this window.

Windows Explorer

Another way of looking at and manipulating your files and folders is by using **Windows Explorer**.

○   Right-click the **Start** button and select **Explore**.

You will see a familiar screen similar to the one you opened from **My Computer**.

Exercises

In this exercise you are asked to create a folder structure which will help organise the computerised files of a double-glazing sales office.

1. Create a folder named **Sales** on your disk. Create two subfolders within the Sales folder. Name these folders **Quotes** and **Appointments**.

2. Create two word processing files and save them in the **Sales** folder. Name these files **Windows.doc** and **Conservatories.doc**.

3. Create the following subfolder structure within the **Appointments** subfolder as represented by the diagram below

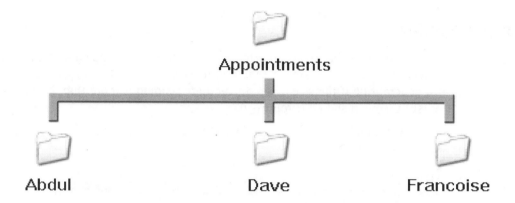

4. Copy the files **Windows.doc** and **Conservatories .doc** to the **Quotes** folder.

5. Re-name the folder **Francoise** to **Francis**.

Working with Files

Compressing files

If you want to send a file as an attachment to an e-mail, **zipping** or compressing the file will make it much faster to send and receive. Some ISPs cannot receive large files. As a general rule if the size of the file you are sending is more than half a megabyte (500Kb) then you should compress it.

Most newer PCs have a program called **WinZip** installed which allows you to 'zip up' files.

Tip:
You can download a trial version of WinZip from www.winzip.com.

- Using **My Computer** find a large file.

- Right-click on the file and choose **Send to**. Then select **Compressed (Zipped) folder**.

In the screenshot below **cat.jpg** has been compressed, and a new folder **cat.zip** appears.

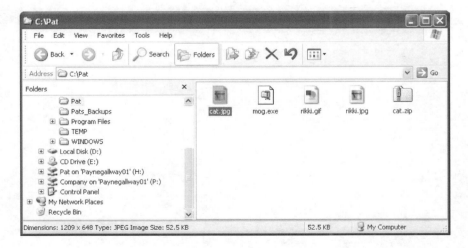

At the bottom of the screen it will tell you how big the current file is. Compare the zipped file with the unzipped file – is it a lot smaller?

Extracting a compressed file

To unzip the file, right-click it and select **Extract All**. An Extraction Wizard will appear, and you can follow the steps to extract the file.

Searching for files

If you lose a file you can use the **Search** facility in **My Computer** to find it again. We will look for **Sharon.doc**.

◉   Open **My Computer** if it is not already open. Navigate to C: and click the **Search** button.

You will see the following window:

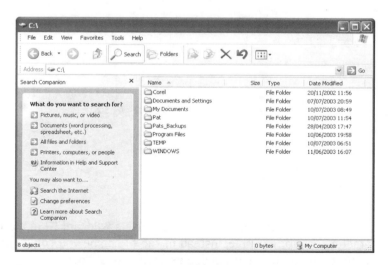

◉   In the box on the left-click on **Documents**.

If you know that you created or modified the document within the last week, say, you can click on the appropriate box.

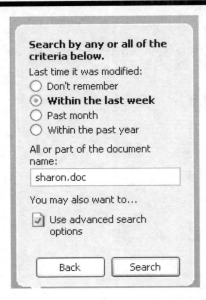

You can click on **Use advanced search options** to search by a range of other criteria such as size.

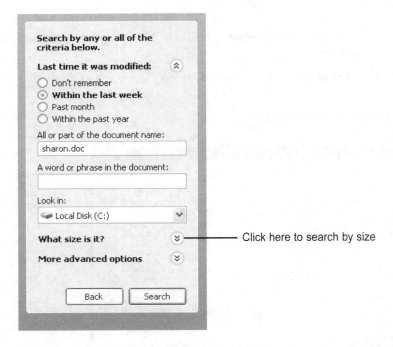

Click here to search by size

If you can't remember the whole file name, you can use a **wildcard** (*) in place of any number of characters. So, for example, instead of the file name you could enter ***.*** to find all files, ***.doc** to find all files with a **.doc** extension, or **sh*.doc** to find all documents starting with the letters **sh**.

You can also search by **content**, by entering a word or phrase in the document in the search box, or by **size**.

○   Click **Search**.

The computer will find the file you are looking for.

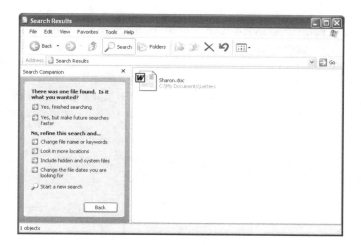

You can open the file in Word simply by double-clicking on it now.

Notice that at the bottom of the screen is a count of the number of files found. You could use this to count all the files of a particular type, by entering say, ***.doc** in the Search box and then searching a named folder.

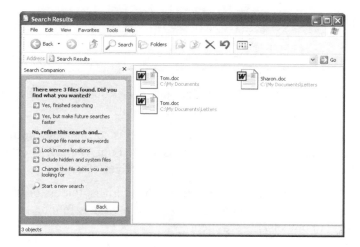

Viewing a list of recently used files

If you want to open or search for a recently used file, there is another way you can do this.

○   From the **Start** menu select **My Recent Documents** or just **Documents**, depending on your computer's setup. A list of recent documents will be displayed and you can open any of them by clicking on the file name.

Viruses

We'll end this chapter with a short warning about viruses, and advice on how to avoid them.

Viruses are small programs developed with a definite intention to cause damage to computer files or, at the very least, cause inconvenience and annoyance to computer users. You should not share or lend floppy disks that could introduce viruses into your system and care should be taken when downloading files from the Internet. Viruses are often sent as attachments to e-mails, so you should never open an attachment that you don't recognise. You will generally see a message similar to the one below when you attempt to open an e-mail attachment.

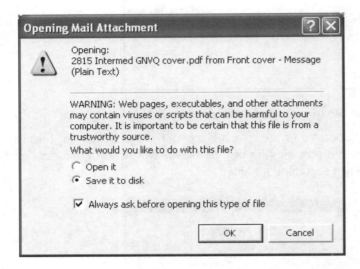

You should take precautions to avoid the potentially disastrous effects of viruses - like some or all of the files on your computer being wiped out.

Virus checkers should be installed on all computer systems so that they automatically check for any infected data when the computer is started up. Manual checkers can also be used to check for viruses on floppy disks, hard drives etc.

Typical anti-virus software enables you to specify which drives, folders or files you wish to scan and **disinfects** the file (i.e. removes the virus) if a virus is found. In this example drive A: (the floppy disk) is scanned.

◗   From the **Start** menu select the **VirusScan** software.

◗   Browse through your files and folders and select which drive, folder or file you wish to scan.

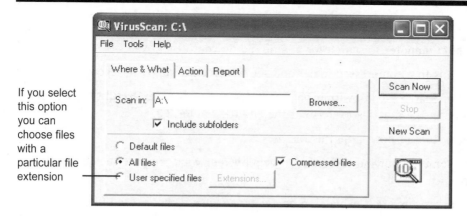

If you select this option you can choose files with a particular file extension

○ Click **Scan Now**.

The software will check all the files on drive A: and report any problems in the bottom section of the window.

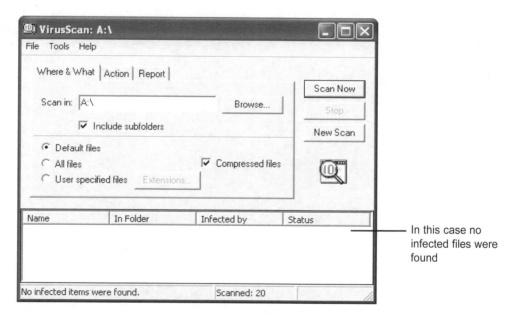

In this case no infected files were found

As new viruses are being discovered all the time the anti-virus software companies issue frequent updates. It is a good idea to install a package that provides an online update service which will send you a message to remind you to update which can then be done online.

Exercises

1. Use **My Computer** to search for a large file on your disk drive.

2. Send this to a compressed folder and see how much smaller it becomes.

3. Use the **Search** facility within **My Computer** to find the file **Useful tips.doc** you created in the practice exercise at the end of Chapter 2.2.

4. Make a note of how large this file is.

5. Enter some text giving three tips to help prevent your computer being infected by a virus.

6. Next enter some text explaining how you can view recently-used files.

7. Edit the document so that each section of text has an appropriate heading.

8. Save and print this file.

9. Use **My Computer** to check the size of this file after the extra text was added.

Managing the Desktop

Creating and removing a desktop icon

You can create a shortcut on the desktop for any program so that you can open it quickly, instead of using the **Start** menu.

- From the **Start** menu select **All Programs** and find the Solitaire program as you did earlier.
- This time right-click the word **Solitaire** and move the mouse pointer over **Send to**.
- Click **Desktop (create shortcut)** from the menu.

A shortcut icon will appear on the desktop.

- Drag the icon into the position you want.
- Try opening the **Solitaire** program using your new shortcut icon. You can then close it again!
- Remove the shortcut by right-clicking it and selecting **Delete**. This removes the icon, not the program.

Tip:
You can also create a shortcut icon by pointing to the file name, holding the right mouse button down and dragging onto the desktop.

Creating a printer icon

It can be useful to have the default printer icon on your desktop so that you can check the print status of any job.

- From the **Start** menu select **Settings, Printers and Faxes**.
- Drag the default printer icon (the one with the tick mark against its name) onto the desktop.

Creating and using a file icon

If you are in the middle of writing a book, say, or a project which is likely to take a few weeks, it is useful to have the file icon on the desktop. You can then open the document in the correct software (e.g. Word or Excel) simply by clicking on the icon.

We'll try this with a document you created in Word.

⊙   Use **My Computer** to navigate to a document, e.g. **Sharon.doc**. Drag the file name onto the desktop.

⊙   Now double-click the icon. The document opens!

Basic system information

It is useful to be able to view basic information about the computer system you are using.

⊙   From the **Start** menu, select **Control Panel** and then double-click **System**.

⊙   Click the **General** tab.

This tells you which operating system and version number you are using, e.g. Windows XP Professional version 2002, Service Pack 1. It also tells you which processor type is installed and its speed, e.g. Intel Pentium III (930MHz). Finally it tells you how much Random Access Memory is installed in the system, e.g. 256Mb of RAM.

This kind of information can be useful if you are reporting a fault on your computer, or want to check whether your computer has the recommended minimum amount of RAM to run a new software package.

Changing the background

If you don't like the desktop background you can easily change it.

○ Right-click the mouse on the desktop picture.

○ In the menu that appears left-click the **Properties** option.

○ In the Display Options box that appears click on the **Background** tab.

○ Scroll down the list and click on a background. You will see a preview of what it looks like.

○ When you find one you like, click **OK**.

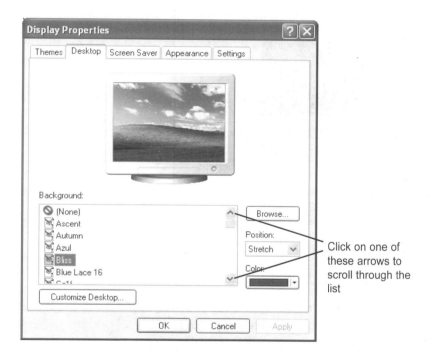

Click on one of these arrows to scroll through the list

Tip:
To scroll up and down a list of items click on one of the arrows on the scroll bar.

Setting up a screen saver

A screen saver is a moving picture or pattern that appears on your screen when you have not used the mouse or keyboard for a specified period of time. As well as being interesting and entertaining these can help protect the screen from burn-out in particular spots.

◉ From the **Start** menu select **Control Panel** and then double-click **Display**.

◉ Click the **Screen Saver** tab.

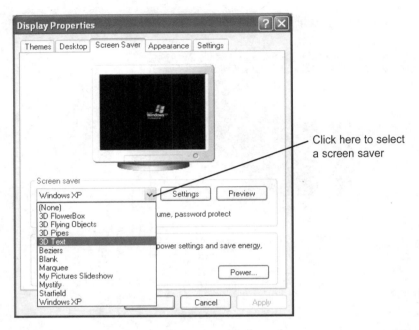

Click here to select a screen saver

◉ Click the down-arrow to view a list of screen savers. Click the **Preview** button to see what the option you choose will look like.

◉ When you have decided on one, click **Apply** and **OK**.

Changing the screen resolution

Screen resolution is the setting that determines the amount of information that appears on your screen, measured in pixels. Low resolution, such as 640 x 480, makes items on the screen appear large and 'blocky'. High resolution, such as 1280 x 1024 makes individual items such as text and graphics appear small but clearly defined.

○ From the **Start** menu select **Control Panel** and click on **Display**.

○ Click the **Settings** tab.

○ Drag the bar to change the resolution.

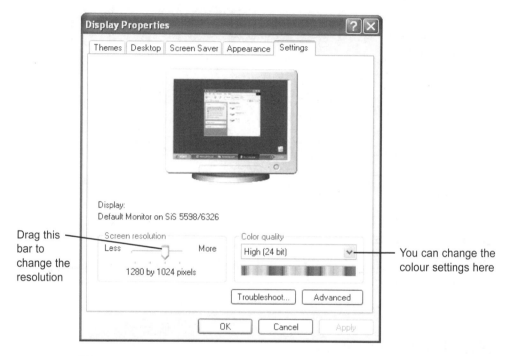

Drag this bar to change the resolution

You can change the colour settings here

○ Click the **Apply** button.

The screen will momentarily go black and then the dialogue box will be redisplayed.

○ Click **OK**.

Other display settings

Using the Display Properties dialogue box **Themes** tab you can set up themes which comprise a background plus a set of sounds, icons and other elements to help you personalise your computer. If you click the **Appearance** tab you can change the appearance of fonts, windows and dialogue boxes.

Changing the computer's date and time

You shouldn't need to change the date and time as it should have been set up correctly for the correct time zone by the manufacturer. However if you do need to it's quite straightforward:

◉   From the **Start** menu, select **Control Panel** and then double-click **Date and Time**. Make any changes in this dialogue box and click **OK**.

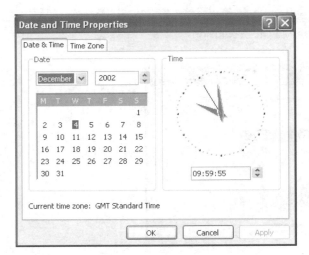

Change the volume settings

◉   From the **Start** menu, select **Control Panel** and then double-click **Sounds and Audio Devices**.

◉   Drag the bar to adjust the sound level.

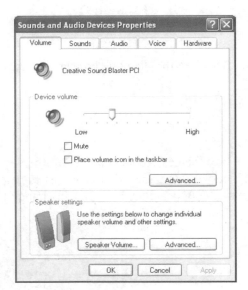

Change keyboard language

Your computer will have a language set as default, probably English (United Kingdom).

If you need to enter text in a different language you can add different keyboard layouts.

▶ From the Start menu select **Control Panel**, **Regional and Language options**.

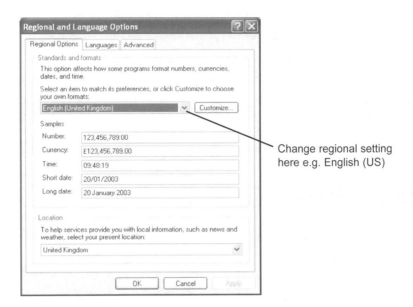

Change regional setting here e.g. English (US)

▶ Click the **Languages** tab.

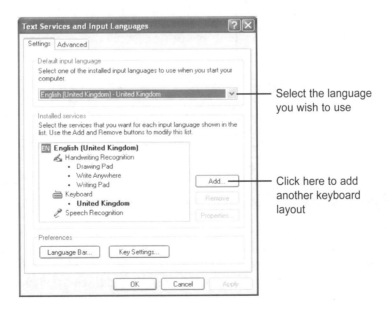

Select the language you wish to use

Click here to add another keyboard layout

Formatting a floppy disk or a zip disk

Most floppy disks and zip disks are pre-formatted when you buy them. However if you need to format one this is the procedure:

 ◉   Insert the disk into the floppy drive.

 ◉   From the **Start** menu select **My Computer**.

 ◉   Click the disk you want to format.

 ◉   From the **File** menu select **Format**.

 ◉   Click the **Quick Format** option and then click **Start**.

You will receive a message warning you that all the data on the disk will be erased and asking you if you want to continue.

 ◉   Click **OK**.

The formatting will begin and you will receive a message when it is complete.

Installing/uninstalling a software application

Most application programs supplied on CD-ROM auto-run when the CD is inserted into the drive and on-screen instructions explain how to proceed. To remove an application program file, it must be uninstalled correctly. Some applications place an uninstall routine in the Start menu. Otherwise you should use the Add/Remove dialogue box in the control panel.

 ◉   From the **Start** menu select **Settings, Control Panel, Add or Remove Programs**.

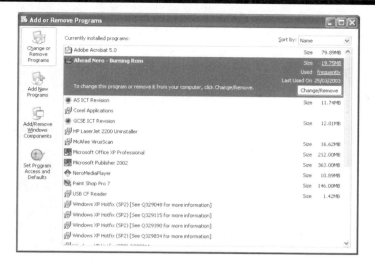

▶ Click on **Change or Remove Programs** to uninstall an application.

▶ Click on **Add New Programs** to install a new application.

The Windows Help and Support Centre

If you have problems with any of the tasks we have covered so far you can always visit the Windows Help and Support Centre.

▶ On the **Start** menu click **Help and Support**.

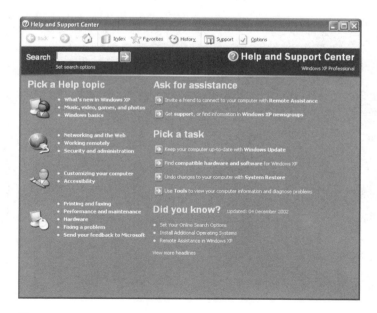

▶ You can either click on a Help topic or type a keyword into the **Search** box.

Each individual application that you run on your computer (e.g. a game, word processor, spreadsheet etc.) will have its own Help system too.

Print screen facility

Sometimes it is useful to be able to take a **screenshot** of what is on your screen and paste it into a document – just as the screenshots have been pasted into this document.

You can either capture the whole screen, or just the current window.

○ Press the key labelled **Prt Scr** next to the **F12** key on the top line of keys on the keyboard.

This copies a picture of the whole screen to the Clipboard. If you now open a new or existing Word document, you can paste it in by selecting **Paste** from the **Edit** menu.

To capture just the current window, press the **Alt** key (to the left of the Space bar) at the same time as pressing **Prt Scr**.

> **Tip:**
> You can see what has been copied to the Clipboard by selecting **Edit**, **Office Clipboard** in Word. This opens the Clipboard on the right-hand side of the screen. Click any item to paste.

Changing the default printer

The **default printer** is used when you click **Print** on the **File** menu of many Windows-based programs. To change the default printer:

○ From the **Start** menu select **Printers and Faxes**.

○ Right-click the printer you want to use as the default printer, and then click **Set as Default Printer**.

A check mark appears next to the printer icon in **Printers and Faxes**.

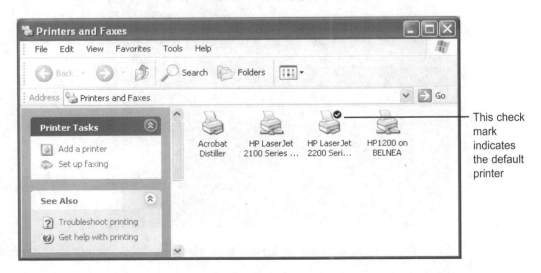

This check mark indicates the default printer

Installing a new printer

Most printers are now **Plug and Play**. This means that you can attach a new device to your computer and begin using it right away, without having to configure it or install additional software. If you are using an older printer it may be non-Plug and Play. In this case you should use the Add Printer wizard supplied with Windows XP.

◐   From the Start menu select **Printers and Faxes**.

◐   In the Printers and Faxes dialogue box, click **Add a printer** under **Printer Tasks**.

The Add Printer Wizard will be displayed.

◐   Click on the **Next** button.

◐   On the following screen select whether you are installing a network printer or a local printer (i.e. directly connected to your PC).

◐   Click **Next**.

◐   Follow through the remaining stages of the wizard: you will be asked which printer port you want to use.

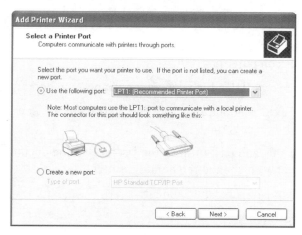

◐   Select a port and click **Next**.

You will then be asked for manufacturer and model of the printer:

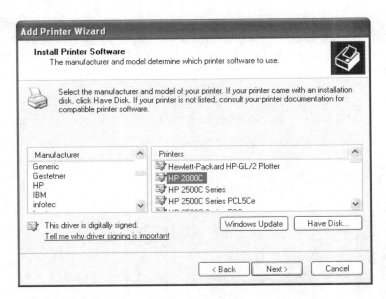

- ● Make your selection and click **Next**.

- ● On the next two screens assign a name to the printer and select whether or not you want to share the printer with other network users. You will also be given the option to print a test page.

- ● Click **Finish** on the final screen to complete the installation.

Exercises

1. Open **My Computer** and navigate to the file **Useful tips.doc.**

2. Create a shortcut to this document on the desktop.

3. Open the document using the shortcut icon.

4. Use **My Computer** to view the Basic System information about your computer.

5. In the **Useful tips.doc** document make a note of the type of processor and amount of RAM your computer has.

6. Now enter some text to describe how you would change the desktop background.

7. Open the **Printer & Faxes** dialogue box from the **Start** menu to view the printers that your computer has access to.

8. Take a screenshot of this and paste it into the **Useful tips.doc** document together with some notes on how to change the default printer.

9. Save and print the word-processed document.

10. Close the file and close Word.